With Twelve

You Get

Goulash

With Twelve You Get Goulash

And other poetic ramblings

Chuck Hackenmiller

Published by Chuck Hackenmiller, former Stacyville, Iowa resident now living in Lincoln, Nebraska.

Editing provided by Debora Duncan of Words Matter Communications, Boone, Iowa.

Printed by Redbrush Publishing Services, Lincoln, Nebraska

ISBN: 978-0-578-90255-5

This book is dedicated to all my siblings and my parents, and to all my aunts and uncles, friends and neighbors who experienced the camaraderie and closeness of being from a large family.

Please use the blank pages inside to record some of your own special memories (by written word or by photos) to share with your children, grandchildren and great-grandchildren and future generations.

This was Visitation Grade School and Marian High School in Stacyville before it closed permanently and prior to when contents inside the facility were sold to the public. Our family was among many that attended classes there through the late 1950s, 1960s and 1970s. The school was later demolished, but the gym/auditorium and kitchen/dining areas in the back of the school were saved and now serve as a community center. Later in this book, I will touch on some Visitation School memories.

Preface

Many people seem amazed when I tell them I'm from a large family; twelve people to be exact. Those who say they have a hard time supporting three children, let alone ten, in this age and era are probably right.

That is why I'm grateful for having such great parents and so many brothers and sisters. All told, today's families are smaller, which makes big families a bit obsolete. Today's high cost of living has much to do with the current 'normal' family size.

Strangers might joke around at the thought of growing up with nine siblings, and I'm always ready for a good laugh, but sometimes my patience wears thin when they say, "there must be a lot of Catholics in that area." Fact is, there were. And my response? "Hey man. My parents are Catholic and they had ten children who are Catholic. That makes twelve Catholics. Now, with twelve Catholics in the family, and the Almighty looking down on us twelve Catholics, maybe He'll give us a group rate break now and then when He passes around His good graces. Who knows, He may give a group travel discount when it comes time to take that chartered bus to heaven."

There are other things I could have said, such as:

"With three children you can only play catch. With ten, you can field a whole baseball team.

With three children, there are fewer dependents on the income taxes. With ten, it's almost exemption paradise.

With three children, if there's a problem, you share it with the other two. With ten children, they each have their choice of someone they think will listen to them."

Obviously, there are disadvantages, too, but those weigh less in importance. Examples? You bet.

At dinner, it's all for one and one for all and "may the best man or lady win" that last pork chop on the serving platter. When a large family gathers around the kitchen table, they gather AROUND the kitchen table.

Arguments developed on long Sunday drives about who got to sit up front with Mom and Dad and who were relegated to the vehicle's rear seats. You knew it was a large family when it took a great deal of effort to remember all family birthdays and anniversaries.

Sometimes it was rough if there was only one bathroom in the house. This was further complicated when we were all in a rush to get ready for school or church. But we survived.

You could go to a family reunion and be called everyone else's name except your own.

When the television schedule showed an NFL game, a classic movie, a favorite TV show like *Bonanza,* or *Lawrence Welk*—all televised at the same time—it was a 'battle of the networks fight' for the channel rights. This happened when there were only three major networks on TV—ABC, NBC, and CBS—with PBS educational television thrown in the mix now and then. I hate to think what kind of battles go on today with so many cable channels.

When one family member got the flu or a cold, it was passed up and down the line. With a big family, you always had to share a lot and that also meant the measles, chicken pox, and other childhood illnesses.

When your former third grade teacher told your younger siblings what you were like in class, it was usually embarrassing, especially if those words reached your parents through a blackmailing brother or sister.

An argument commonly occurred among my sisters when the morning, noon, and evening dishwashing chores arrived. The mêlée was usually settled out of court when a firm reprimand from Mom was the final ruling.

Imagine the family was going on an outing, and after traveling 30 miles down the road, the folks asked if the last one out of the house shut off the kitchen light. Nobody ever knew whether they were the last one leaving the house.

It was laughable to our parents when the party line would ring and all ten children came running to the telephone at once, each claiming it was their call.

Whether coming from large families or small families, it was important that each member was there for the others, through both troubles and happy times.

And there were a lot of happy times with our family. Holidays and other celebrations were merrier. Maybe that's what this nation needs more of today: more family togetherness. It can be difficult to hold in pains or hurts, joys and good news, if there is no special someone, like a sibling, to share those emotions.

During my childhood years, one guest at our home made the comment that she, "had a friend who stayed at another friend's home for a few days." The home where her friend stayed had sixteen children, but it wasn't until the second day of the friend's visit that the father of that large family noticed there was an extra child seated around the supper table.

He laughed; everyone laughed. It was one big, happy family.

I can see that happening. I lived it.

List your parents and siblings, and tell what you liked about big families?

Chapter One

Summarizing the Blessings

Let me sum up what I can recall about big families and living on a small farm in rural northeast Iowa, based on what I've seen, heard, smelled, tasted, and felt.

Things I've seen. Little baby chicks scattering to the back of the brooder house when someone entered their domain; a hanging tree branch moved by the wind, touching the electric fence and causing a spark or two and sharp snapping noises; sparkling white snow under the yard light during and after a blizzard; a view from the silo top as far as the eye can see; a Sunday chicken dinner spread, with the drumsticks sticking out atop the serving plate; a grove of trees bowing as thunderheads and gale-force winds crept up on a once-sunny day; soft lights glowing through the barn windows when winter's eve darkness arrived, and again when Dad began milking the cows at the break of dawn; frozen cow pies in the cow yard that were always an obstacle when pushing the milk can cart to the milk house cooler; a perfectly stacked and squared load of hay; Dad sliding down the elevator from the hayloft after the last bale was unloaded, sweating profusely because of the summer's high humidity; a garden full of produce that could feed a multitude for a full year.

Things I've heard. Soft footsteps downstairs in the wee hours of Christmas morning; Dad snoring on the couch during a lazy Sunday afternoon, the newspaper at his side; the putt-putt sound of the old John Deere tractor as it rolled through the farm yard; water running into the empty cow tank; the jingling of chains and grinding of gears on the mounted corn picker; crickets chirping on a sultry summer evening; cars in the distance coming down our gravel road; Mom listening to local radio personalities during the morning hours, to catch up on the local community news; barking dogs and hissing cats sparring with each other; the cackling of chickens while gathering the eggs; the crackling sound and sporadic bright sparks as Dad welded iron in his workshop; the clanging of milk cans hauled on the two-wheel push cart; the sucking sound a calf makes when it reaches the bottom of the milk pail; neighborly conversations; Lowell Thomas and the CBS Evening News or a Minnesota

Twins baseball game during the evening milking chores; the setting of dishes and silverware on the dinner table; loose change making noise in Dad's pockets.

Things I've smelled. The Sunday delight of chicken baking in the oven; popcorn after it's been popped and poured into Mom's huge bread-baking bowl and doled out to each child into smaller bowls; hay the day after it's been cut; leather from brand-spanking-new shoes; the rubber smell of new five-buckle boots; manure, with each pen for cows, pigs, or chickens carrying their own distinct odor; perspiration from the bands of sweat-stained seed corn hats; the fragrance from our lilac tree; freshly-turned sod in the spring when preparing the soil for planting; singed hair from butchered chickens; backed-up sewer or septic tanks; fresh milk and cream straight from the milk can; a pet dog's breath; the starting of the oil furnace for the first time each year; freshness from the pine trees; incense from Holy Week and Easter church services; hot steam puffing from Mom's iron; the lovely scent of a real Christmas tree; a soiled oily or greasy rag in Dad's workshop; fresh corn or hay silage; leather from a well-worn baseball mitt; exhaust fumes from the tailpipe and hole-filled floorboard of our old International pickup truck.

Things I've tasted. Mom's fried chicken and homemade bread; ice cold water fresh from the milk house pump; hard candy from Mom's journeys to rummage sales in neighboring Iowa and Minnesota cities; blood from pulled teeth after one of many visits to the dentist; bland soybeans fresh from the field; juicy clover or weed stems growing in the pasture; beef liver or pork brains, definitely an acquired taste; desserts sneakily stolen from the basement freezer; yucky liquid cold medicine; beverage refreshments and desserts shared with neighbors while taking a break during those hot harvest days; fresh green or red tomatoes straight from the garden; freshly picked juicy plums ; sour green apples; corn on the cob; a candy bar purchased at the Stacyville Co-op Elevator; broken-off icicles dangling from the eaves of the garage roof; grilled hot dogs or hamburgers; homemade jellies.

Things I've felt. The tightness of violin strings; fur of the dog who rubs up against my legs; manure chips stuck on cows; the softness of a baby kitten; the ruffled neck of a young calf; a very short haircut—called a butch—after Mom retired her clippers for the day; gripping pebbles on a brand-new basketball; the strings or laces on a new baseball or football; the sharpness of Dad's pocket knife; a baby sibling's soft skin; scabs from cuts and scrapes;

stepping on a nail or glass; the roughness of new shingles on a roof; touching a steaming kettle without potholders.

It doesn't stop there. My parents had ten children, so they had an extra sense—a sixth sense of sorts—about everything necessary to help push or steer their children in the right direction.

What are some of your favorite holiday memories?

Forever a Family

What is it that tightens the bonds
between parents and their children?
What draws families close together
and keeps the lines of communication
open?

The answers can be found in single words,
some that all parents might want to learn.
And if they take these words to heart
there will be fewer heartaches or
concerns.

Dedication. Happiness. Tenderness.
Patience.
Sympathy. Caring. Understanding.
Enduring. Gentleness. Innovative.
Honesty.
Kindness. Praising. Cooperating.

Talking. Listening. God-fearing. Sharing.

Playing. Working. Insight.

Feeling. Listening. Compassion.

Responsible.

Fairness. Reasoning. Foresight.

But the most important word

that ties all of these words together

is none other than the four letters of love,

which makes family memories last

forever.

Chapter Two

Living Big

Recently, at a corner table at a fast food restaurant, a man, woman, and two teens were dining together. The two adults were having a spirited conversation while the two teens were preoccupied with their electronic gadgets, pushing buttons with one hand while consuming their food with the other. Neither child looked up and had a conversation with the other throughout the meal; each instead had their eyes glued to their tiny screen as they focused non-stop on whatever game or texting they were doing.

Welcome to the technological advances of today's world. To some it has its merits, because in a fast-paced society everyone, including my own family—through cell phones, apps, computers—is seeking an edge over the competition.

This wasn't true in the childhood era of the 1960s and 70s, when an early rising and daylight hours mixed with hard work, and sweat was all the working edge a person needed.

Rarely was there enough money available among large, rural families to dine out. At mealtime, what was on the home dining room dinner table had to be shared equally by my parents and their ten children. Most of the items on the table were freshly made. Nourishment came from Mom's homemade bread, vegetables from her garden, and the meat from home-butchered hogs, cattle, or roosters.

There were never enough chairs to go around the table, so Dad made a long, pine bench to complete the seating arrangements.

Many times, many years ago, the conversation around the dinner table was similar to countless other nights. Most of the gossiping, ridiculing, or rehashing was laid out in the open, the talk usually initiated by my parents.

"Did you do well on your tests today?"

"Don't drip ketchup all over your nice shirt!"

"What do you mean you had to stay after school and clean the chalkboard and clap all the erasers clean because you were acting up in school today?!"

"Leave that last chicken drumstick for Dad; he worked extra hard today."

Eventually, all ten children chimed in, tattling about something naughty their older or younger siblings did, which prompted scolding from our parents. The children talked about homework assignments, upcoming events, unique ideas, and then argued about whose turn it was to do the dishes when the meal was over. They talked about achievements and what they wanted to do when they grew older. The youngest to the eldest all had their say.

Getting a word in edgewise required patience. The best opportunity to speak was while the fresh, warm dinner rolls were being passed around. Everyone's mouth closed as their eyes focused on Mom's mouth-watering rolls, and most of us were too spellbound to engage in any conversation.

With twelve hungry mouths around the table, mothers—and their daughters—had to be creative with their entrée selections. Meals had to stretch. That meant that hamburger from the home butchering, for instance, had to be served in a variety of ways at different meals throughout the day: patties, loose meat sandwiches, casseroles, meatballs for spaghetti, or blended into numerous other soups or dishes.

And then, of course, there was always goulash to fall back on.

My family had a lot of conversations over plates of goulash. Simple to make in big batches, it was a cheap fix, except at times when, as a special touch, the noodles were made from scratch, with chunks of home-grown tomatoes stewing inside the covered pot.

It might have been, while downing a forkful of goulash, that siblings mentioned what college or careers they were hoping to pursue.

There were serious discussions, or what we interpreted as dire words, that transpired while the steaming kettle of goulash was being passed around the kitchen table.

What didn't get eaten was usually recycled into another meal the next day, or fed as slop to the hogs. That never happened with Mom's goulash, oozing with noodles and plentiful chunks of beef. The serving dish was empty, our plates appeared to be licked clean, and stomachs were content.

Often with twelve around the table there weren't ample leftovers to store in the fridge, unless it was liver and onions, cow's tongue, pig's brains, or beets; they weren't too popular with most of my siblings or me. Each of us had to sample it all, though, or there would be no dessert.

What a way to sway a child to clean their plates! Sweets were hard to resist. There was always a dessert to go with the noon and evening meals, like baked-from-scratch cakes, pies, or cookies, considerable helpings of custard or rice pudding, forkfuls of apple strudel, or luscious caramel-cinnamon rolls, waiting in the wings. We realized at an early age that each cringing chew of cooked cabbage, fried pork liver, or fried parsnips would be rewarded with a sliver of sweet-tasting heaven.

Yes, we siblings and our parents devoured lots of goulash, in addition to plenty of other comfort foods like chicken or beef casseroles, pancakes and eggs, homemade bread, and whole potatoes that were sliced, diced, or mashed. It's those meals that fill today's pages of locally-published recipe books from schools, nursing homes, club organizations, and more.

With each helping, warm conversation occurred around the table, and in the years that followed, had us yearning for second helpings of treasured sweet, or bittersweet, memories of growing up in a big family.

What were some of your most memorable family meals?

Chapter Three

The Pecking Order

No doubt about it: walk into ninety percent of homes today and you will find what might be considered a 'family museum'. Metaphorically-writing, a majority of these family artifacts, or art pieces, are hanging on the walls or attached with magnets, clinging to refrigerator doors or message boards.

On those walls, among the clicking or chiming clocks of all shapes and sizes, you might find varieties of plaques trumpeting children's past accomplishments in school or sporting events, floral arrangements purchased from home sales parties, that huge, stuffed walleye caught while someone was almost half asleep in the boat and ready to head to shore, the mounted talking fish or deer heads that little children can't resist hearing over and over again, a shadow box filled with wee items provoking neat memories that 'tell who we are', perhaps some art that came straight off a garage sale table (considered to be a rare find), a shelf collection of corn husk dolls, an encased old razor blade Dad used when he was in his twenties, a thimble Mom used in her sewing kit, a sculpture that sparked a conversation, or a rustic art piece or cloth, covering a gaping hole produced by a misguided hammer.

But none of these can hold a candle to the sacred hallway wall of family history. On display are viewings for all generations, a so-to-speak pictorial family tree, meticulously and strategically aligned, that displays either black and white or digitally-mastered colored photos.

One might find close-up pictures of parents or grandparents, personal wedding photos of yesteryear, and baby photos. These 'scrapbooks on the walls' then evolve to photographs of the children's graduation from high school and college, more weddings, grandchildren, and so forth, until it's time to expand onto another wall.

If families were large, there might have been some serious contemplation about adding on a new wing, just to accommodate all of the pictures.

Some sixty years ago, my parents started their hallowed wall of generations with a picture of their firstborn, a professional photo of a baby girl whose crib shared the same bedroom as her parents. Above the crib was a bust of the Blessed Virgin Mary, a comfort to Mom and Dad knowing Mother Mary's praying hands watched over their child's every move.

In the years that followed, nine more shared that same sturdy crib.

Sue, then, was the oldest of ten. Next came the red-haired Ruth, and in August of 1954, the first boy in the family—myself—emerged and found a spot on that wall of baby pictures.

In retrospect, after reflecting on my baby photo, it seems apparent that I had no future in farming, like my father. After all, I was dressed in a faded, bluish shorts held up by black suspenders, sitting up and looking like a writer. There were no farmer's bib coveralls on me, and I had a sheepish smirk on my face that disguised an attempt at drooling at the extremely patient photographer who was likely holding a cookie or a squeaky toy, to get my attention. As roly-poly as I looked, I probably preferred anything food-related over a plastic rattle, in order for the photographer to get my attention and smile.

In the following order came more baby pictures on that memorable family wall: Elaine, Alan, Frank, Marilyn, Ann, Doris, and the youngest of the ten, Mary.

Mom said a majority of our first names, chosen after birth, were picked "because it was just something she and Dad liked." No, Frank wasn't named because of Sinatra, the name Marilyn wasn't picked because of Monroe, and Doris wasn't named after Doris Day. However, Mom said that the youngest, Mary, was named after Bing Crosby's daughter, Mary Frances. Middle names for the boys, she said, were named after saints. Mine was Joseph; Charles Joseph Hackenmiller.

On that note, she and Dad were probably saying, "What were we thinking, giving them saintly middle names?!" This was said, upon reflection, of the harrowing task of raising their three boys and seven girls.

Once all my siblings grew out of the baby crib stage, they had nowhere to go but up in our two-story farmhouse; that is, all the way upstairs to the top floor bedrooms. Unless a child was ill with the flu, or needed monitored medical attention, nobody who was not a baby or wee toddler slept on the first floor with our parents. If any of the children were sick, their place of evening rest was the downstairs living room couch.

On the upper floor were three bedrooms. The girls were afforded the largest and second-largest of the three bedrooms because there were more of them, while the boys made themselves comfortable in the smaller room. I and my brothers had a very small clothes closet. It should have had a sign posted on its entry door just like the rides at the amusement parks: Not for anyone taller than five feet.

For the boys, it wasn't so important to have a gigantic closet space because we could usually stuff, through selective cramming, most of our clothes in dresser drawers. Nobody knew what they'd find in those drawers on cleaning or laundry day—maybe a candy wrapper or food remnants from a late-night snack stolen from the downstairs refrigerator. My sisters tell me they detested cleaning our room; some looked on it as a scavenger hunt.

Usually the oldest of the girls had their own room, for privacy's sake. Once one of the siblings graduated from school and left the nest, room arrangements were changed.

Each bedroom had its treasures, in one form or another. Once, by surprise, I stumbled on a box of caramel-flavored 'diet candy' in one of my sisters' dressers. I think I was searching for a book. The candy was advertised to suppress appetites and it was the latest fad among teenagers at the time, and I wasn't a teen yet.

Understand: no way was I a deprived, malnourished child. But this boxed candy was like a mouse catching the scent of peanut butter—irresistible and all too tempting.

The more of that candy I ate, though, the fatter I got. I should have written the company and requested a refund. After eating handfuls, I obviously never lost any weight, but it did give me stomach pains and eventually lessened my appetite.

So, I guess it did suppress my eating habits, but only for a short time. I was back raiding the refrigerator hours later.

I heard record players blaring music, and some dancing going on, in those rooms, when the girls had cousins or neighbors over for the day.

That biggest room upstairs had a closet that held lots of secrets and mementos from Mom and Dad that might make a collector drool. Inside were items from play days long ago; Dad's violin, with some strings detached, antiquated holiday decorations, old board games, and interesting knick-knacks were all explored by all siblings on rainy days.

As key inhabitants of the upstairs domain, we were barred from downstairs whenever Mom and Dad entertained evening guests, usually card parties with neighbors or our aunts and uncles. None of the siblings could see what was going on, but it was obvious there was fun in the house that night. The smell of our uncles' cigars drifted to the top of the stairs mixed with the aroma of fresh-brewed coffee. Laughing was loud and contagious around the card tables below.

We had our own fun going on upstairs. My sisters played their board games; my brothers and I got out the rubber band pistols or blooper ping pong ball guns, taking aim at targets in our room, trying not to hit each other.

The girls also played with their dolls, listened to records, or we all played our own games of cards, called *War, Crazy Eights*, or *Go Fish*.

We read our books when lights were out, aided by a faint gleam of moonlight shining through upstairs windows. Some of us would leave the comforts of bed and sit by the hall-way nightlight, to get in a few more chapters, which is probably one reason why so many of us needed eyeglasses or contact lenses later in life.

There were many memories made in those upper rooms, but Christmas upstairs was special. All of us stayed wide awake on Christmas Eve night, thinking we'd hear a noise like a thud from Santa Claus dropping or dragging his bag, or as he chugged his milk and crunched his cookies. All was silent.

On Christmas morning, however, none of my siblings wanted to wait in their room. Instead, we gathered in a huddled mass near the top of the stairs, pushing and shoving each other for every inch of room to race to the downstairs furnace grate. On a cold evening or morning nothing compared to the warmth of that floor furnace, even as the grate indented the flesh of our feet.

Ahh, but Christmas. Ready to bound down the stairs, as we always did when we awakened on bitter cold winter mornings, patience was at a minimum until the oldest sibling gave the command from atop the staircase.

"Go!"

No need to hear that command twice! We rumbled down the stairs, seemingly flying, missing two or three steps on the way down. Once we all reached the Christmas tree, it was a free-for-all. Ribbons were tossed aside and wrappers flew in all directions. Decorated boxes, once holding gifts of toys, clothes, or candy, were smashed. It was over in fifteen minutes or less, but it was quite the spectacle and extremely exhilarating. Some years the gifts were plentiful; some years they were lean, but all of us got something to unwrap and treasure.

It was a few minutes of joy, followed by the rest of Christmas Day, enjoying our gifts and cleaning up the mess, or preparing for the holiday feast. Each room of our house couldn't hold back the aroma of Christmas dinner preparation. I can still taste the chicken, gravy, sweet potatoes, mashed potatoes, and desserts.

Christmas music filled our home. The girls took piano lessons and were talented in playing and singing. The ivory keys on the piano were never worked as hard as they were during the holidays.

There was no need to frost the windows for Christmas decorating. Where we lived,

Mother Nature's frigid country air took care of that. The fresh scent of our live Christmas tree infiltrated all corners of the old house.

Every holiday card, unlike greeting cards today that pop up on social media outlets, received by my parents or other family members would be taped to door frames and around our living room entrance. Many of the cards contained personal notes of how family members were getting along, of the past year's accomplishments, and best wishes for the New Year.

Cable television was non-existent then, but our television set was not deprived of Christmas shows and musicals. There were many *Lawrence Welk* holiday specials on the TV, and the reruns of this waltzing and musical show still bring back great memories today.

The many guests joining us for Christmas celebrations helped make the season jollier. Even all the uninvited guests, such as the pet dog or cats that squirmed through an open door, couldn't resist the cozy, homey atmosphere.

One year at Christmas I was sick with a high temperature. I wasn't very old and Santa Claus was still very real to me. I was resting on the couch when suddenly there was a rap on the entry door; three times I think. I darted from the couch and bolted to the house entry door, not wearing socks or shoes at the time.

On our outside steps was a heap of Christmas gifts. And here I was, walking barefoot around in the snow, forgetting momentarily about my sickness. It was a better cure than all the medicine that I'd been given!

Sixty years ago, there were many other families with ten or more children in and around my home town and other parts of the county. Sometimes it took three hands to count, by fingers, those other families' children, and even harder to remember all of their names.

Do the math. It wasn't always a bed of roses for my parents or those other families to raise ten or more children. There were many mouths to feed, lots of clothes to buy, and tubs and tubs of clothes to wash and hang to dry on the outside clothesline, in summer and winter. There were school tuition bills to meet and other bills to pay. With only one bathroom in the house, patience—and privacy—regularly ran thin. Mom labored endlessly, baking numerous loaves of bread on Monday to get us through the rest of the week. She also washed and hung huge laundry loads. Dad worked hard to produce a crop and keep the dairy, or other livestock operations, running profitably, just to pay the bills.

Don't overlook the advantages, though. Those many little 'exemptions' came in handy at tax time. When it was chore time, if one child was sick, there were plenty in the wings to take the ill one's place. We could also field a whole ball team in an intramural softball tournament.

We had our own pew in the town's Catholic church, as did many other parishioners, and we filled it up, too, every Sunday and on holy days. To this day, we can form our own church choir and sing at church services.

There was plenty of help available when picking and cleaning the sweet corn, butchering the roosters, or harvesting the fruits from the garden.

In later years, as the children grew, the family always seemed to have an in-house babysitter—an older sibling—and plenty of cooks who learned the tricks of the trade from Mom. No automatic dishwasher was needed with so many working hands available. Wash days went faster with more hands to help, although the loads increased dramatically, weighing down the outside clothesline and using up the bag full of clothespins.

There were more birthdays to celebrate, more wedding dances to attend, and more potluck reunions to enjoy. Sharing on the farm was not a virtue, but a necessity. Treasured items, such as older siblings' clothing, toys, or tools, were passed down from one to another until they were either unwearable and turned into farm rags, or became scrap for the junk pile.

I guess I'd have to say, also, that when the Good Lord preached, "Bless all the little children," those blessings came to us in abundance, because there were so many of us. Indeed, those blessings were counted every day when we recited our evening prayers before going to bed.

You could bet that the walls inside our home were covered from one end to the other with family photos of blessed events that meant so much to all of us. We siblings can look back now on those photos and remember, with gratitude, what our parents and grandparents brought to the table for us.

Today, we live in a technological-driven and mobile society. People relocate to different areas of the country or state because of family ties, jobs, or other ventures. Some never find inner peace and wander the earth, searching for that place they want to call home. That inside peace might come in different shapes and styles: a mansion with multiple bedrooms and bathrooms, a small cottage on an acreage, or whatever is affordable.

So, a definition of home has narrowed to being with family, and an abode is not limited to a place of shelter with a roof. No matter what house you live in, home is where you want to hang your hat. Within its walls, it houses memories that are far too many to erase.

What do you remember most about the features of your family house?

Home is Where the Heart Is

Those first few days are unbearable

in surviving the first true test

of being such a long distance away

from the family nest.

Social media may make the miles shorter

but it still isn't quite the same.

Missing are familiar sights and sounds.

In all honesty, is being homesick such a
shame?

There are so many reminders.

A home-cooked meal. The holidays.

Crickets outside the window. A song.

Resemblances of home seen in many ways.

This is when it's time to reach
for that inner strength to look ahead.
What has passed cannot be changed.
Hold onto those memories instead.

Pursue those goals and ambitions
and take everything in stride.
Learn to appreciate the home
and those feelings carved inside.

So that, again, when thinking about
what is treasured but still so far apart,
remember, home is just a beat away,
found within the heart.

Heavenly Decorations

Look beyond colorful Christmas lights
and lift your head up high
to gaze at the infinite number of stars
sparkling brilliantly in the sky.

There is no earthly decoration
that matches the twinkling star
seen on a calm, cloudless evening
beyond the horizon, stretching far.

These heavenly objects before you
are what astrologers love so much.
But in admiring the star-filled ceiling
you will find other things stars touch.

A peaceful feeling is ever present
within hearts captured by the sight
of the vastness of the starry universe
glowing down on the world at night.

So when, at Christmas or anytime, you
try to find the spirit of the holiday,
seek the heavenly formations of stars
as laid out in God's special way.

Take the time to stargaze
when the wintry night sky appears full.
You'll have no regrets in doing so
because it does wonders for the soul.

Chapter Four

Amen to That!

It was a ritual that continued throughout our childhood, immediately following the evening meal and before the night milking chores commenced, once the last drumstick from the entrée plate was consumed.

All twelve family members would scatter from the kitchen table, where dirty dishes were still piled high, and dash to a bracket hung on a nearby wall. The bracket had several hooks, each one holding a coveted rosary.

The rosaries appeared in all sizes and shapes, dangling loosely in the hallway. Mom's rosary was the pretty glass-beaded one held together by a small silver chain. Dad's rosary was black, the heavier beads made of wood. Each of the ten children had their own, the plastic beads held together by string or chain. Some rosaries glowed in the dark. Many of our rosaries were obtained as gifts from First Communion or Confirmation. A few might have been in disrepair or frayed, but still faithfully served their purpose.

Most times, the older children lit a devotion candle at a station away from the table, arguing about who would get the matches to set the wick on fire, a task sometimes complicated by the wick being buried deep in the wax.

Then began the hectic scramble for the kitchen table chairs to lean on. "Nobody gets that chair!" and "That's Mine!" were echoed simultaneously. Chairs for rosary reciting seemed to be a necessity, because for a good, long time we knelt on our hard, unyielding, linoleum-covered floor. From start to finish, through the five sacred mysteries, knees and backs sometimes got pretty stiff. Leaning over on those chairs while kneeling was such a comfort. Those unfortunate enough to not have a chair had to resort to leaning against another piece of furniture, such as the kitchen table where the table scraps were in full view. On frigid nights when the temperatures dipped into the teens, some fought for kneeling turf next to the floor furnace.

All family members took turns each night at being the rosary leader, from oldest to youngest. All learned their rosary prayers such as the Apostles Creed, Glory Be, Hail Mary, and Our Father, through religious lessons at Stacyville's Visitation Catholic School, or through constant repetition. Saying those prayers six days a week, 52 weeks a year, obviously helped us remember each solemn word. Monday through Saturday, about twenty minutes each day, or a half an inch shorter on the wax candle, was devoted to the rosary. Monday, the leader recited the Joyful Mysteries; Tuesday, the Sorrowful Mysteries; Wednesday, the Glorious Mysteries; the cycle repeated itself on Thursday, Friday, and Saturday.

Sunday was a day of rest from the rosary, most likely because it was substituted by the hour-long obligation of church services in town.

Each rosary leader had his or her way of leading the rosary. Dad, at times, would be swift because he knew the cows were waiting in the barn, ready to be milked. Mom's recitation was more pious. My presentation was slow and deliberate, because I wasn't in a hurry to venture outside into the frigid cold and complete the evening chores. Some siblings were articulate in leading the prayers, some not. After all, daylight was fleeting. The responses to the prayers were always concise and in unison.

Once the last prayer and final "Amen" were recited, the younger children would bolt to the devotion candle, to be the first to blow it out. Wax dripped down the side of the candle and sometimes got on our clothes. I liked to put my finger into the hot wax and let it harden on my fingertip. It actually felt therapeutic.

Sometimes we'd have a change of venue and move into the comfortable, carpeted living room to say the rosary, especially during Advent or Christmas Eve, where the homemade crèche sitting atop the television set was the center of our prayers. I recall one prayer session on Christmas Eve when, just as we said our last "Amen," a rap came on one of the living room windows. It wasn't a "ho-ho-ho," but we had an inkling it was Santa Claus. Once we finished recitation of the rosary, all the children rushed out the door and saw a pile of gifts on the outdoor step. One of my sisters, who was sick with some sort of flu bug, had a miraculous recovery and was giddy and prancing outside in the cold and snow, trying to find her gift.

My only questions were, "How did Santa know exactly when the rosary was finished?" and "Exactly how long was he looking in our window so he knew when to knock?"

So where did that daily recitation of the rosary get us? Did it make us more saintly?

Likely not, because immediately afterward my sisters were yelling and screaming, threatening each other about whose turn it was to wash and dry the dishes accumulated on the table, and my brothers and I still slacked off on our chores, which at times got us in trouble.

We would steal leftovers from the refrigerator or freezer, especially Mom's cookies, or we would break curfews when we got older. Even Dad still swore, until his face was beet red, at the cattle now and then.

Mom, however, stayed true in faith to the rosary, never straying from its powers. That simple twenty minutes of daily prayer and unity helped form the heart of our big family, which keeps beating even though my siblings are spread out in many different directions. Today, Mom still confides in her beads as a sanctuary for the protection of her children, grandchildren, great-grandchildren and friends and, every once in a while, she would get in a prayer or two for her own causes.

Not only the rosary, but any prayer would do in a pinch. When I was about eight, I had my very first birthday party, and all my neighboring friends came over to help me celebrate. One of the gifts I got from my parents was a brand-spanking-new Louisville Slugger baseball bat and a rubber-coated baseball. Granted, it wasn't an official, cowhide-stitched baseball, but nonetheless, it was round, firm, and traveled far when it was crushed off the new bat.

Almost too far. That day, to my chagrin, with one mighty swing the baseball soared into a weedy, thorn-infested ditch along our country road. At that time, Dad didn't want the county spraying the ditches because they contained some blackberries that Mom wanted to harvest and bake into jellies or pies.

After a lengthy search by me and my buddies, I was resigned to the fact that my new baseball was gone, swallowed up by the earth, never to return again. It saddened me greatly.

Mom, in her infinite, prayerful wisdom, didn't give up. She insisted I pray to St. Anthony, patron saint of lost causes (or for that matter, lost items), and perhaps a miracle would occur and the baseball would reappear. So, I did just that. If anything was a lost cause, it was me…right?

Did I find the baseball immediately afterward? No. No miracle arrived that soon, but several years later as I was wandering in the ditch on a fall day before winter's arrival, there was a round object sitting amongst some weeds. Sure enough, it was my rubber-coated baseball, a little worn from the seasons and caked with dirt. It was like finding buried treasure.

Once a year, Dad's fraternal organization, the Catholic Order of Foresters, would make an annual trek to a radio station in Decorah, Iowa, where they took turns reciting the rosary over the air waves. They even took me along one year. I don't know how much praying I concentrated on at that time, because being in a recording studio and seeing all the radio operating equipment and microphones intrigued me greatly. We got through it all without incident and, on the way home, stopped at a restaurant for treats and to recount the experience.

I'd conclude that it was the rosary that bonded this family together—on its knees, with or without chairs—because we were leaning on something even more comforting: the power of prayer.

What did you do on Sundays with your family?

Visitation Church in Stacyville.

He Listens

When we search high and low
for a way to escape life's pains,
we'll find the answers somewhere, but
not in substance, nor monetary gains.

We'll encounter rocky roads that often
cross the devil's path.
So, it's a great comfort knowing that
never alone do we face evil's wrath.

Because there is One so mighty that,
even through the darkest night, He sees
and lifts the burdens from our souls,
to help us find solace and put us at ease.

He fills our emptiness with
compassion, understanding, and hope.
His arms are willing to gather us in
when we're given more than we can cope.

As the spirit weakens and we wonder
how we can survive,
He feeds us the strength necessary
to believe and keep our faith alive.

To find Him, look not outward;
He's always closer than your touch.
Call upon Him often, never give up.
No matter the struggle, it's never too
much.

God listens to all, knows all,

and He'll give you a brand-new start.

If you talk to him in a prayer

that comes totally from the heart.

A family ride with siblings in a grain
wagon, pulled by my dad Rudy.

Chapter Five

Home Advantage

We were blessed to have a multitude of activities on a wide-spread, 140-acre farm whenever chores could wait or were completed for the day. Favorites included playing ballgames in the backyard, with cousins or with neighbors who resided within a walking distance of a half mile away or further.

At our house, we'd grab our taped-up wooden bats and ball gloves, find the closest field venue, and pick sides. Then we'd set the bases…the scrapped, round disc blade would be first base, an old burlap feed sack would be second base, and the telephone pole with the basketball hoop attached to it would be third base. Home plate would be a bare patch of lawn near the lilac tree.

The ground rules were simple. Balls hit into the ditches along the county road were fair game, even if they landed in a thicket of prickly cockleburs and berry plants. No sympathy was allowed for a bad bounce on bumpy ground that smacked someone in the nose and caused excessive nose bleeds. Anything hit over the tall trees and across the gravel road, into a makeshift centerfield or a neighbor's field, was considered an automatic home run because the outfielders always had to look for cars before crossing the road. The two tall ash trees standing side by side in centerfield rendered power hitters useless unless balls went through the branches or cleared the tree tops. Right-handed pull-hitters would hit balls into the tall grass in a small field and leg out extra bases because fielders couldn't locate them. Hitting to the right side meant the ball could be hidden somewhere in the garden amidst Mom's tomatoes or potatoes. Fielders had to be careful not to smash Mom's peonies, carrot tops, or radishes.

We'd play until parents, aunts, and uncles said it was getting too dark to see the ball, or they had to be heading home, or we had to start the milking chores. After all that, we'd still play some more.

Road games in the shadows of night were fun, too. After milking chores, the family clan would bike or walk south or north on the county gravel road and play in a neighbor's backyard, which had a whole new set of ground rules regarding protection of house windows and vehicles.

Another away ballfield to the north featured an actual leftfield barnyard fence that served as a homerun barrier. Hit a ball beyond the fence and you might bean a cow, or maybe the ball landed smack dab in the middle of a cow pie. That's why it was an automatic homerun: it took too long to clean the ball at the closest water hydrant.

How many ball games can you recall when action had to be stopped to chase a loose calf back into its holding pen, or the seventh-inning stretch included a quick serving of beverages and cookies by hosting parents? We had a lot of them.

There were times, however, when nobody was around for a ballgame because most were working in the fields or visiting other relatives. So, on other lazy Sunday afternoons when Dad had some free time, he'd grab the potato pitchfork hidden in the crevices of the toolshed and begin digging for earthworms or juicy nightcrawlers, which usually could be found around the spilled grain near a farm building, or underneath rocks or boards stored against shed structures. We helped break up the clods he dug and, bare-handed, pulled out the slimy, wriggly worms and dropped them in an old coffee can. Throw in some dirt and grass clippings and we were set, with all the bait we needed.

Dad would load up the fishing rods that were stored on rafters inside the garage, and then put the poles in the trunk of the car, or in the back of the pickup.

There was no need for precise casting of lines; it was simply a matter of dropping a line in the water near the riverbank, or letting it float downstream with the current. The water was never more than twenty yards wide.

Often, we'd go to a fishing hole along the winding Little Cedar River near Stacyville. Dad would park the vehicle in a field driveway and we'd walk along fence lines and tall grass, or crawl under a fence, hoping not to catch a sleeve or trouser leg on the barbed wire while we ventured toward the riverbank.

There, we baited the hooks that hung from the lines of the hodge-podge of poles. Some of the siblings used cane poles, or parts of one, to dip lines and bobbers into the water. Those who were more coordinated used rods equipped with reels. The Little Cedar River's banks were filled with a lot of brush on both sides, so when casting, we had to be careful not to get lines tangled or hooks caught on low-hanging branches or tall grass. Mostly, however, standing along the bank with so many of us fishing at once, the trick was not to snag each other's floating fishing lines and get them hopelessly tangled.

We caught our share of bullheads, maybe some bluegill or crappies, while Dad relaxed on the grassy bank and listened to his battery-operated transistor radio that was probably carrying a Minnesota Twins baseball game. He was interrupted often, mostly to use his pliers to dig out a hook swallowed whole by the crappie or bullhead, or to untangle messed up reels and release hooks and lines from greedy, outstretched tree limbs.

As it got toward late afternoon, and images of bobbers going up and down were etched into our memories, it was time to pack up and return to the farm for the evening milking chores. But before nightfall, Dad would skin the bullheads and clean them so they'd be available for a meal or two on the following days. He made cleaning fish look so easy. The smaller, nonedible fish, alive and well in an old bucket, found their way to a new life in the cow tank.

As I entered my teenage years, I grew fonder of Dad, who I decided had more patience than anyone. That's because when I took one of my little sisters fishing with me one afternoon, I found it was no picnic. It was her first time and all she wanted was to haul in the supreme, almighty, never-seen-before, humongous fish that lurked deep in the waters. She declared that she'd bring in the fish, but emphatically said I had to pull out the hook so she didn't have to watch or touch it.

The air around the river had a fishy smell to it. Probably, somebody decided to clean their fish at the exact place where we were going to wet our lines. Flies were buzzing all around us so we moved elsewhere down the Little Cedar River and found a cozy spot with a cool breeze. I grabbed my own pole, baited my hook, and tossed it into the river, and did the same for my sister. Then I turned on my transistor radio and listened to the game, wondering how Minnesota Twins baseball players Harmon Killebrew and Tony Oliva were doing during a contest at Metropolitan Stadium in Bloomington.

A rap came on my shoulder. "Help me," she said.

"To do what?" I asked.

Apparently, she had pulled up the line and noticed her worm had escaped. "I don't like to kill worms and they are dirty, too. Girls aren't supposed to get dirty," she added primly.

I told her I'd do it one more time, but the next time she had to bait her own hook. Once that was done, I headed back to my resting place and had almost dozed off when she tapped me on the shoulder again.

I looked up and she was holding her pole, but something wasn't normal. Her line was strung into a nearby tree, looking a lot like a spider web. "How in the heck did you do that?" I asked.

"It just happened," she said.

If it wasn't my second-best pole, I'd have called it a day and let it ride. Instead, I climbed the tree and felt every poking branch as I untangled the line bit by bit. There were knots that not even a Boy Scout could tie, and the hook was snared on a pine cone. When I came down from that tree, I was exhausted.

She'd lost the worm, of course, so I baited her hook again, against my better judgment. Then I begged her to be careful.

After twice more losing hooks to snags in the river, and breaking a line on unyielding rock, she began getting the hang of it. That was after she thought she was stung by a bumble bee, only to realize that she had stuck herself in the arm with the hook.

I got in a short nap but was awakened with a cry. "I caught the first fish!" she bragged. Oh, the fish wasn't any bigger than the bobber, but it was her first catch and she was excited.

With all the hullaballoo, I forgot about my fishing pole, which had been dragged into the river. "You should have been watching your fishing pole like you told me. Now what are you going to fish with?" she asked.

Grrrr. Patience, they say, is a virtue. That day, it was more of a trial.

But with large families, patience is required more than ever. How my parents could be so patient, with ten children pulling at them with their every whim, is remarkable and hard to understand. That is, until the children have children of their own, knowing that the next day will be better, that the next fishing line tossed into the river might bring in the biggest catch of the day, and that waiting for a good pitch will help you hit the ball high over the centerfield trees.

What fun family activities did you do?

My Dad

He didn't waste words.

Mostly went right to work.

Never one to idle. Always there

where responsibilities lurked.

His days of early risings,

blisters showed through on tattered
gloves,

laboring long into weary night hours.

It was his way of showing us love.

But I remember the dad

who put a worm on my hook

on a sunny, lazy Sunday

near the rush of a babbling brook.

I treasure the memories

of he and I at play,

How he showed me how to trap gophers,

digging mounds at sunlight's first ray.

He made stilts or other playthings
during rare times that he was free,
or shared salted peanuts to
satisfy hungry gazes from me.

He'd let me milk the gentler cows
while he tackled the ornery, unsettled
ones.
He opted for the harder, tedious chores
and left easier ones for his sons.

He cared, he labored, he wanted
his children to achieve.
Soft spoken was how he wore his love,
loudly for us to hold, and believe.

Mom's Tribute

Millions of women can qualify.

They easily possess the proper

credentials.

She may never receive an award for her
merits

even though she fulfills all basic essentials.

Their struggles often go unrecognized

for the many achievements that they do.

It's not always the headlines they seek

but satisfaction from all the little things,
too.

Like taking the scraped hand of a wounded
child

and wiping away the flowing tears.

A little first aid and a kiss to the hurt

turn a saddened face to cheer.

She takes the time to watch the child
participate in athletics or the county fair.
But oh, never criticize the child's poor play
or else she'll knock you off your chair.

When a child loses interest
and the urge to learn and motivate,
she will not pursue and pressure for her
benefit,
but instead has the patience to wait.

She'll make the child eat properly
no matter how the dish is hated.
A clean and empty plate of spinach
is what made her so elated.

When a child strikes out
or blows a line in the high school play,
there's nary a hint of disappointment in
her face
because she knows that there will be other
days.

Her many occupations come with no pay.

A nurse, cook, mediator, delivery gal, or
spouse,

accountant, housekeeper, production
supervisor,

or psychologist—all without leaving the
house.

Inside she finds resourcefulness in

a child's messy piece of art.

When a note of piano music is off key

she still brags about her little Mozart.

She appreciates grocery store bargains

so the children can enjoy vacations,

or likes to save for life's important things

like her child's wedding or college

education.

This woman is no ordinary person

and cannot be replaced as easy by   another.

The woman who dedicates this life to a
child

has always been known to us as Mother.

Maybe we can lavish them with gifts,

to let Mothers know we care.

But sometimes all it takes are the words,

"Thanks Mom, for all the times you were
there."

What do you remember most about your mom and dad?

Chapter Six

Transportation Mode

Through the years, my parents had their share of used vehicles, both cars and trucks.

Country living required having a functioning vehicle so we could travel and purchase daily necessities, or transport us to and from key destinations, be it a trip into town for groceries or the feed mill, to church services or schools, or to visit grandparents, relatives, and friends. I wish I had the bill of sale on each of our parents' cars, just to compare to the cost of today's models.

My fondest memory of a vehicle driven by Dad was a green-colored International pickup truck, a late 1940s used model that he and I drove off the lot from a dealership in the county seat of Osage, Iowa. Inside the cab, the mileage odometer read well over 100,000 miles. It wasn't the type of vehicle that Dad wanted to use to bring the family to a Sunday church service. This was an old, bulky, barely functioning, working man's truck. However, at the time it seemed like a brand-new vehicle to me.

As a child, I was fascinated by the interior's gizmos and frills, although they were just a fraction of the features and wizardry that today's vehicles carry.

It wasn't automatic transmission; it had a stick shift on the steering column that would pull in and up for reverse, pull in and down for first, push out and up for second, and straight down for road gear. Three on the tree.

The maximum speed the truck could travel without considerable shaking was probably around 65 miles per hour. We were never in a hurry with it anyway.

The window wipers were the most intriguing. A knob high above the dash, above the driver's head, turned clockwise and operated one wiper, then another half turn and both wipers would work, emitting a whirring sound like that of an electric egg-washing machine, as the skinny wipers glided back and forth. The wipers moved at one speed.

The push starter, to turn over the truck's motor, was on the floor, to the left of the clutch and brake pedals. When the truck was difficult to start, there was a choke knob available on the dash to help it along.

Some of the accessories attached to this green workhorse truck were built by Dad as he formulated his plans from scratch, such as the tall sidewalls and enclosed tailgate of the truck bed that would be used for hauling grain to the town elevator, or for hauling cattle or hogs to and from the sale barns or the nearby meat lockers. The whole pickup, when pulled ahead from the livestock chute, would rock back and forth; the farm animals were obviously restless on their journey out of the driveway and on gravel roads to the butcher or livestock auctioneer.

Once the truck's mechanical parts began rusting, the transmission started faltering, and it became too dangerous to drive on the open road, part of the vehicle was reincarnated.

My brother and Dad used their welding skills and converted the truck bed into a small, two-wheeled trailer that could be pulled by a tractor, filled with grain or ground feed, and backed into small, hard-to-reach places inside hog buildings or barns.

Still, the pickup wasn't the oldest vehicle on the farm. An old, black 1940s car parked on wooden blocks rested underneath the shade of an apple tree, occasionally bearing the beatings of fallen apples on a windy day. I can't recall if it was a Chevy, Ford, or Plymouth, but it was one of my parents' first cars. My oldest sister had a harrowing experience in this vehicle in the days when it was in road-ready condition. She fell out of one of the four doors while it was moving slowly on a gravel road. No injuries occurred, but there was momentary panic from the parents.

There were other trucks and cars that my parents owned that transported the whole family to locations throughout the county. One of them was a 1960s Plymouth station wagon, deep red in color. On a typical trip to our grandmother's house, our parents were in the front seat, with the smallest sibling stuffed between them. The middle seat had room for at least four or five younger siblings, and the large back area of the station wagon had space for the rest of the clan, the place of highest demand because of all the room back there.

The red station wagon met its demise in the late 1970s when, during a downpour, I crashed the front end into a stalled vehicle that was stopped on a busy state highway. The other driver had stopped to pick up a fallen tailpipe. On that day, I and three other riders were coming home to the farm after a school day at a Mason City business college. The car that I hydroplaned into carried a woman and some children. Nobody was hurt or ticketed, but it was frightening to all involved.

As the siblings became grown adults and left the farm, there was no need for larger vehicles so more practical sedans of all colors came into the picture: a car that was bright yellow, nicknamed by my brothers as 'The Canary'; a dull brown Plymouth Satellite; a silver Dodge. Some of these cars were passed down to the children as they went off to college, or were driven by siblings until they could afford their own car, or until the wheels fell off.

Eventually, we siblings were able to purchase our own used cars; some came with high mileage and were on their last legs. Siblings that had longer trips to make regularly bought vehicles with fewer miles.

I bought my first vehicle when I was 18; it had originally belonged to a hometown cop who used it for his patrol car. It was beyond the century plateau of driven miles, but it was something that I could call my own, and it came at a cheap price. The blue Plymouth Fury had a push-button transmission; the buttons were located on the left side of the dash. The car's top had leftover bolts that used to hold a domed police light, used to stop mischief or speeding motorists, or more likely to lead a parade.

When that car wore out in the 1970s, my next used car was a Ford Galaxy, and financing it included my first encounter with a bank loan officer, who advised me on how to pay the loan back at $65 per month. I equipped the car with a citizen band (CB) radio, which was the craze at the time, one that I wasn't about to miss out on.

My identification, or handle, in CB jargon was 'Super Scoop', which tied into my early journalism career. I bought the car from my newspaper publishing boss.

The CB came in pretty handy and it was great talking to the truckers on the highways, or friends who had their own 'handles' and knew CB terminology. The speedometer eventually gave out on the Galaxy, so the CB was extremely helpful when driving on four-lane highways like I-35, on the way to the Twin Cities. I'd pull up next to a fellow CB'er, aware of the antenna they had clamped on the trunk, and I'd ask—and get an answer—on how fast they were going so I could follow at the same speed and not be caught speeding by highway patrolmen often frequenting the busy interstate.

A Plymouth Duster was my next purchase, bought from my brother, who had upgraded to a newer car. The greatest accessory in that vehicle was an eight-track player; I could listen to rock band music by Bachman Turner Overdrive, the Doobie Brothers, and others while coasting to and from work.

I didn't buy a brand-new vehicle until the 1980s, after I was married and had children of my own. It was a mini-van, but I didn't have to squeeze ten children into a vehicle like my parents did, only three at one time.

I'm wondering: how did we ever squeeze twelve people into one vehicle, and why didn't we notice how crowded we were from front to back? How did we entertain ourselves on the longer trips?

I'm guessing there was just a lot of talking, and a whole lot less listening, plus plenty of room for laughing, in that little red station wagon, all the way to and from grandma's house.

What cars, trucks or tractors did your family and you drive when you were growing up?

Coming Down the Road

Who is that building a cloud of dust
on the gravel road that passes our farm?
Is it the county grader, working the gravel
to keep travelers from accidents or harm?

Is it the mailman, carrying letters
from someone who loves to keep in touch?
Perhaps it's the milkman on the dairy
route.
Really, the suspense is just too much.

Maybe it's the neighbor pulling a wagon,
as our ears strain to pick up a sound.
What if it's unexpected dinner guests
when there isn't ample food to go around?

It could be that bright yellow bus,

bringing children home from the school day.

What it could be is the ice cream truck,

making its deliveries along the way.

There's a chance it's the veterinarian,

called to get livestock on the mend.

Or this could be a fast-talking salesman,

eager to show off all the latest trends.

Eventually, the mystery passes on by.

Life returns to what it was before.

That is, until more dust appears on the horizon

and sends us guessing just once more.

Chapter Seven

Bed Rest and Soda Pop

There were numerous health advantages of rural living, with the availability of fresh fruit from the apple trees, fresh vegetables from the garden, wide open spaces of fresh air, plus exercise-inducing chores and activities that bolstered our muscles and heart rates.

But the guardian angels had their hands full with big families. Nobody was immune from sickness like the flu bug, fevers, earaches, tetanus infections, rabies, strep throats, broken arms, accidents with machinery, or other misfortunes.

If one of the ten children became ill with the flu, it would spread to all the others in the family. That meant, perhaps, a day or two of sleeping on the couch, watching television all day, and getting some special care and attention from Mom. Some days we'd be given a respite from school, but had to make sure that we had a signed note from our parents to our teachers, telling them why we weren't there at the classroom roll call.

Rest, and a cloth smothered with a warm nasal-cleansing salve, wound around the neck, did wonders; adding a few aspirins normally helped in the recuperation. Dad would be sent into town; he'd come home with bottles of soda, such as Royal Crown Cola, Ginger ale and Frostie Root Beer, which would settle the upset stomach.

Sometimes that still wasn't enough of a cure and an appointment had to be made to see the family doctor. The doctor's office had a distinct scent, a medicinal smell only a physician's office has. Once the nurse led me to Doc's office, with Mom right behind, the nervous waiting began.

Then the 'miracle man' walked in, his white coat gleaming and not a single hair out of place on his head. His sweet-smelling hair tonic made sure of that.

The first thing he did was place a flat stick on my tongue. He'd say, "Say Ahhhhh," and he'd scour the back of my throat for any unusual blemishes on my tonsils. Nine times out of ten it was a virus making me ill, and several times I left the office rather sore because of the antibiotics that were injected by needle into my posterior.

Now the sight of that long needle and the thought of pending soreness would traumatize many a child, but most knew that the country doctor had a trick up his sleeve, and it came out of his treat drawer. Waiting inside was a stack of strawberry or grape-flavored suckers, to ease the pain or dry the tears of a sobbing child. I was sick often in the elementary grades. In third grade alone, I missed about ten days during the school year, and although there were some days when temptation rose to play hooky, I never did.

As a young lad I liked climbing trees. However, one misstep on a branch had me crashing to the ground and led to a visit to the doctor, where x-rays revealed a broken arm. The arm was reset and a cast was made, and for weeks I wore it as a badge of honor, showing it off to cousins and neighbors and having it autographed.

The scariest part of it all, however, was the cast removal and the nightmare of seeing a circular saw above my arm. With precision, the physician split the cast in two, the smell of Plaster of Paris penetrating the air. I was so relieved to see my arm intact, with no scratch on the recovered arm, once the sawing was done.

Dental visits also were part of the family's wellness routine. Most of my siblings were prone to cavities because, as our parents would say, "we enjoyed having some cereal with our sugar."

We had sugar on our toast, sugar on our strawberries, and we indulged in the many desserts offered to us. Payback, of course, was a trip to see the dentist, where we'd cringe at the sound of the high-pitched drill, or fight through the numbness of the Novocain that helped us endure the procedure.

I was one of the ten children who had braces on my teeth, so my dental visits were frequent. What a relief it was to have the metal braces removed! Retainers were offered by the dentist, to keep my teeth in line, but I usually shrugged them off, often hiding them at home in hard-to-find places, against my parents' wishes, such as my dresser's sock drawer, or inside a beer mug that was part of the kitchen and dining room décor.

As much as we all loved walking barefoot through puddles and mud on the farm, it wasn't always a good idea. Nails or glass would sometimes be where least expected and would often find their way into the bottom of some-one's foot, hence forcing iodine on the wounds, or stitches for the deep cuts. Tetanus shots were a must!

We also had to be on alert for strange-acting animals that could be carriers of rabies. The animals could be stray cats, dogs, rac-coons, or even cows bitten by rabid animals. My youngest brother had to undergo a series of painful rabies shots after being bitten by a cow. Harm's way extended throughout the farm and none of the family was immune from it. Daydreaming while on the job wasn't wise; in fact, it was downright dangerous.

Electric fences were all over the farm to keep the cattle from straying into other fields or neighbors' cornfields. Many of us were jolted by the wires as we crawled under them and popped up too quickly. Sometimes, the wires needed to be tested to see if the electric fence was doing its job. That required strategic placement of screwdrivers or other shock-proof items onto the wire, which would cause a bright spark, a procedure that should never be done on a rainy day.

As toddlers, we were not allowed to go across the gravel county road; a fenced-in yard served as a deterrent for that. However, we siblings always found a way to get in harm's way. As a toddler, I crawled out from under the yard fence and journeyed down the gravel road, where a passing motorist picked me up and took me back to the farm, asking Mom, "Are you missing somebody?"

Dangers came when operating farm machinery, always calling for alertness and an eye for details. There were always risks associated with clothing catching on grain augers or tractor power take-offs; tipping over implements and lawnmowers while driving on steep inclines; unclogging the hay from balers; unjamming the stalks from corn pickers.

Peril also appeared while using silage un-loaders, shingling the steep roofs of houses and sheds, scaling the towering silos, and attempting to maneuver through muddy fields.

And using pitchforks.

Dad and I were cleaning out the dairy barn's calf pen one fall day when, at the same time, we both threw our pitchfork loads of manure into the spreader. The next thing I knew, Dad was gripping his forearm, blood sluicing down to his fingers, and he streaked immediately from the barn to the house. He didn't scream in pain or unleash a well-deserved scolding. He had been impaled with one of the tines of my pitchfork.

The doctor, Dad, and Mom worked extremely hard to fight off the resulting infection, and he was very, very sick. It was the longest he had ever been bedridden. My Mom, brothers, and sisters all kept up with the chores while he fought off the infection, but all the while, I suffered with remorse and anger about the mishap, blaming myself.

Luckily, Dad recovered and went about the business of being a father and leader to his family, not once mentioning the incident to me or indicating any wrongdoing on my part. The best part was, he still would share a stick of chewing gum with me, take me to town with him on errands, and play catch with me when the milking chores were done. It was as if nothing bad had ever happened and, for that, I was very grateful. Because, for what was ailing me at the time, that was the best cure I could ask for.

When you were sick, what care did you get?

Heroes

Most often, idols of
arrogance, selfishness, and greed
sneak into our presence, blinding
us to the heroes we truly need.

Why look into the realm of glitter
when heroes exist nearby,
as close as someone's touch, hug,
or a wipe of teardrops from the eye?

A hero can be a parent or a friend who
guides you through struggles and strife,
or a partner that loves you dearly
every single minute of your life.

Perhaps the hero is a teacher, who offers
more than scholastic wrongs or rights.
It could be a person who listens,
understands,
and steers you toward spiraling heights.

Heroes then, are not always
the famous, the richest, the strongest,
but can be people we often overlook—
those who stand tall by us the longest.

Chapter Eight

Kindergarten Roundup

*T*his old man, he played one,
   he played knick-knack on my thumb
   with a knick-knack, paddy whack,
give the dog a bone,
this old man came rolling home.

This old man, he played two,
he played knick-knack on my shoe
with a knick-knack, paddy whack,
give the dog a bone,
this old man came rolling home.

This old man, he played three,
he played knick-knack on my knee
with a knick-knack, paddy whack,
give the dog a bone,
this old man came rolling home.

And so it went, on and on, at least ten
verses of the old man rolling home. It was
probably the very first song that I memorized,
other than, "Twinkle, Twinkle Little Star" and

"Mary Had a Little Lamb." I have kindergarten to thank for that.

As a family on a farm, we learned many things. When you call the cows home with a high-pitched sound, they know it's time to leave the pasture and head for the evening milking. The sun will rise in the east and set in the west. A hay rack will hold much more than 80 square bales if it is properly stacked.

You can't trick a laying hen to leave its eggs unguarded in the straw-filled nest; let's face it, they will furiously peck at you. You know exactly how many shovels of corn, oats, and bags of feed additives it takes to grind a good mix of hog feed.

Obviously, sharing reduces arguments, especially when you're dividing the last piece of pie into equal parts. It's wrong to rile roosters in wide-open spaces because they'll come after you. Never be the last one to use the last sheet of toilet paper and not replace it, and always put the lid down. Treat Holstein bulls with utmost respect and never, ever turn your back on them. Remember to plow a straight furrow. Don't wear your chore clothes in the living room or school clothes into the barn. Don't spit against the wind and don't light the burn barrel on windy days.

You just didn't forget those things.

However, all of these real-life learnings didn't prepare us on how to print the alphabet, use proper sentence structure, pronounce words, calculate adding and subtraction, keep in pitch at music recitals, get along with other people other than our own family and neighbors, and take short afternoon naps on a shaggy rug. That's why we needed school. And kindergarten, for most people, was the first place to start.

Since my family resided in the country, a bus delivered my siblings and me to and from the doors of the kindergarten school, which in this case was in St. Ansgar, Iowa, about 15 minutes from our home.

Bus transportation was a priority when school districts covered miles and miles of territory. Weeks before school began, the bus drivers would practice driving routes so there would be no trouble on that first day. The trusty drivers stopped at the end of driveways, opened their doors with the amber caution lights flashing, waited a few seconds, then moved on to the next farm on their list when nobody showed. Practice made almost perfect.

On that first day of kindergarten, excitement abounded as Mom stood with me at the end of the driveway, at least for the first day of classes. She would send off many of my siblings to kindergarten as the years passed on. The bus rolled up with its yellow, then red, lights flashing, and in my case, the motherly bus driver pulled the silvery handles on the door and invited me in.

I can't remember if I was too shy to sit with another child, or if I sat by myself, but I remembered how that bus driver always looked up at that mirror above her to make sure everyone was safely seated, and then moved on to the next stop. I recall that the ride on the gravel road was bumpy, and even rougher when riding in the back of the bus, on washboard gravel roads.

There was no mischief on the bus because one stern look from the driver's eyes, reflected in the mirror above her, was louder than any punishing words.

On my lap, in my little school bag, that first day were the required essentials: brand-new eight-count crayons, pencils with erasers on them, a small lunch bag filled with homemade snacks, and an old, rolled-up, green shaggy rug to nap on.

Honestly, those lessons I learned in kindergarten must have stuck with me, and I must have passed into first grade without anything holding me back. All those memories aren't crystal clear after all; it's been close to 60 years since that first bus ride.

There were other snacks offered throughout the day. I recall some timely milk and water breaks that helped us focus on our lessons and not obsess about how hungry we were. I vaguely remember the recesses and some of the activities inside the classroom. My kindergarten teacher, who also taught most of my younger siblings, was very motherly and very patient. That was a good trait for someone dealing with the likes of 20 or more six-year-olds in one room.

Oddly, what I most remember is the nap time after we had snacked. We pulled out our rugs from designated areas of the classroom and found a spot on the floor to rest our heads for about a half-hour or so. I could never sleep; I just kept thinking about food, I guess. Or perhaps I was too anxious for the next recess, or how straight I could draw my letter L, or how to write my first name. The room was quiet and gave the teacher a nice break and time to plan for the next activities.

We created gifts for our parents, such as our handprints absorbed in clay; or colored pages where we actually "stayed within the lines."

Another memory was about the program we put on for our parents in the spring. I vividly remember the song and the sticks I had to rap together to keep beat with the music.

This old man, he played six,
he played knick-knack on my sticks
with a knick-knack, paddy whack,
give the dog a bone, this old man came rolling home.

I smacked those sticks so hard I thought I'd broken them in two. The audience was captive and appreciative; the applause was sweet.

One final memory of kindergarten came on a day when I most likely had neglected my rug nap again and was daydreaming too much. At the end of the school day, I was evidently feeling pretty tired, probably because I was trying to tackle how to write my long last name of Hackenmiller.

The bus pulled up and the bus driver smiled as she opened the doors. I went straight to an unoccupied seat in the rear of the bus, and that bumpy ride must have made me doze off a little, probably dreaming about knick-knack, paddy whack and wondering if I had a bone to give to my dog before the old man came rolling home.

It was, however, not the bus driver's fault as she pulled to my home's driveway and nobody got out. She undoubtedly looked at that mirror above her and didn't see me anywhere. She likely thought I went home with my parents earlier that day. So, she moved on. How was she to know I was dreaming about sleeping on my little green rug, sprawled on the bus seat, hidden from her view?

Mom told me she had her bus route about finished when she found me sleeping on the seat and had to come all the way back to the farm and drop me off.

I guess that kind of put a scare into me, too. Afternoon naps came few and far between as I grew older, but now that I've approached the Social Security jet set, I find myself seeking out something that reminds me of those comforts of a cuddly rug and blanket for an afternoon snooze, and I don't feel one bit guilty.

What can you remember about your very first day of school, or riding on the bus?

On Their Way

We're certainly proud of you, child.

My, you have certainly grown.

You're heading for another milestone

in the world, all on your own.

Smiling, I can recall

those first words as you talked.

Then came teeth and favorite toys

and nasty spills when you first walked.

But I feel slightly saddened

and I feel a little like a fool,

as we walk together, hand in hand

to your very first day of school.

I know beyond those doors, child,

is a place where you can glue

pieces of what you wish to be

and make it all come true.

From building blocks, hunks of clay,
to learning the alphabet,
it's only the beginning of molding a future
toward education goals you will set.

Perhaps I'm over exaggerating and
putting the cart before the horse.
But why, when I let go of your hand
do I feel a certain twinge of remorse?

Likely it's because I hadn't expected
the time would come so fast
when I'd be watching you leave
those toddler years in the past.

Give me a hug, child. Your teacher awaits.
I'm choking for advice to say.
"Why the tears?" you ask inquisitively.
"Cause, my little one. You're on your way."

Shoestrings

With determination, wee fingers grip the

shoestring,

gingerly struggling with escaping knots.

The thumb, sore from pressing, stops
hopes from slipping away,

twisting the bunny ear loops, as

concentration heightens.

There will be other days to pretend. This
test is for real.

Breaking the ties of dependency, leaping to

independence.

The final tug. No unraveling. No loose
ends. A masterpiece created.

A cocky smirk shatters the tension.

Fragments of childhood float away.

It's easier crossing the stepping stones in
life

not having to worry about tripping over
loose shoestrings.

Chapter Nine

Making Do

There were items we were able to live with, and some we had to do without. It was mostly what could be afforded at a particular time and place.

Mom was a baker, and a very good one at that. On baking day, it wasn't uncommon for her to bake twenty or more loaves of bread, in addition to dinner rolls, cookies, cinnamon and caramel rolls, apple coffee cake, pies, and numerous other desserts. She would freeze a lot of it for future meals.

To make all those breads, coffee cakes, and sweet concoctions required a sizeable flour bin, one that held twenty-pound bags of this precious dough-making ingredient. Her bin was built into a kitchen cupboard, rarely empty because she took advantage of advertised grocery specials on flour.

Mom never needed a written recipe to make her bread; it was all in her head. She learned from the best, her mom, who also raised a large family of three boys and five girls, and was an excellent baker, known for her cookies and pastries. It was always a treat to go to grandma's house because we knew there would be wonderful sugar cookies waiting for us.

Experience and repetition were all Mom needed to have her loaves come out perfect almost every time. "This much flour, this much yeast, makes this much dough," she would say. "Knead it and watch it rise. Put it in the oven and watch it bake."

If we were lucky, we were given a taste test during Mom's bake fest. We'd beg for the warm bread, smothered with a spread of butter and cinnamon sugar, or homemade jelly.

Bread was a common staple in our big daily meals. To top the wonderful taste of bread was the, sometimes hand-churned, butter made by whoever's turn it was to turn the crank on the churn. The chore of churning normally fell to the younger ones in the family as it took a good share of the afternoon to get it to the necessary texture, and the older siblings had other chores to finish.

The milkman, who daily picked up our full milk cans from the previous morning and night milking, would also fill our weekly orders of fresh, one-pound blocks of butter. Before the milkman arrived in the morning to haul away the milk, we'd open up the milk can and skim some cream off the top, an ingredient essential to Mom's baking.

Homemade jellies, made of rhubarb, strawberries, apples, raspberries and blackberries, huckleberries, gooseberries, peaches (that came in the mail), plums, and other fruits, were sweet toppings spread generously over the bread. There were many arguments among the siblings about who would be lucky enough to get the crust, or butt, of the homemade bread. We'd fight over that just as hard as battling for that last chicken drumstick.

The main meat entrée on the dinner table, whether it was a roast of pork or beef, also came from home. Our parents butchered at home from a choice of their own fattened livestock, or we transported the hog or steer to meat lockers in nearby towns, keeping the large freezer in our basement full for months with a hefty meat supply. The roasts, steaks, pork chops, sausages, and hamburger often were on the tables for the noon or evening meal. There was little waste. Liver, pork brains, and tongue were delicacies treasured by some, but mostly by Dad. Bones were saved and used for soups and then tossed out to the dog. Even the rendered fat was used to make lye soap.

Dad and Mom would purchase sausage casings and, by using an old grinder, would spend time in the basement making sausage bologna rings, an event usually done on a rainy day when fieldwork had to wait.

We sometimes caught fish, usually catfish or bluegills from the Little Cedar River, and fried them up in Mom's cast iron skillet. I recall meals of pheasant and rabbit, too. There was really nothing my Mom couldn't cook.

Every year we butchered roosters that we raised from mail-order chicks, and froze the meat for later to be fried or baked, usually for Sunday noon meals or special occasions. Gravy, almost never lumpy, was made from the meat drippings, ladled onto heaped helpings of mashed potatoes, the spuds dug up from Mom's spacious garden. Potatoes, carrots, peas, beans, and other vegetables always had a spot on the dinner table. Canned pickles, either dill or sweetened, also came from the vegetable patch. So, a typical meal might have all items provided from the home front, with the exception of condiments like ketchup or mustard, salt and pepper. Some families had extra horseradish and would share with their neighbors.

The reward for consuming all that food was a generous helping of dessert, made by Mom and my sisters. Cakes and cookies were made from scratch. Pies, too, filled with home-grown apples, strawberries, rhubarb, huckle-berries, blueberries, and raspberries, tasted wonderful with either homemade ice cream or five-gallon pails of ice cream bought from a local delivery service.

The large, tall glasses of milk came from our own dairy operation. Eggs from our own henhouse were gathered by my siblings and me, then cleaned for our own consumption. Some were crated and sent to a local store in town.

But enough about food. There were numerous other ways to remain thrifty and still have enough money left to make a Sunday contribution to the church.

Mom and her friends often made Friday or Saturday day trips to nearby bigger cities. What they hoped to find were bargains at area rummage sales for shirts, dresses, jeans, jackets, or coats that they could give to, or remake for, their own children. That saved each of them the expense of buying new clothes, especially coats and jackets, for the younger ones. Many of the clothes were purchased for nickels on the dollar, which helped make their precious dollars stretch.

Special occasions called for new clothing and shoes, however. Those big events included first communions, confirmations, school programs, or the first day of school. "Try these on," Mom would say as she guided us through the department store. She always knew right where to go. For me, it was always the department store's husky section for pants and the larger shoe sizes.

My siblings and I still uphold the garage sale traditions, looking for practical items or finding treasures from yesteryear. Nowadays people, including some of our family, enjoy going through antique malls or yard sales to find something to repurpose, such as an old table, to give it a new life.

Each year communities continue to have city-wide rummage, garage, or white elephant sales and my siblings and I don't shy away from them. The bumper sticker, "WE BRAKE FOR GARAGE SALES!" certainly applies to us.

It wasn't just the women that couldn't resist bargains. Dad and other local men attended farm auctions and came away with used implements or livestock accessories at prices much less than newer model prices, depending on the bidding.

Not a lot of time was spent at the hair salons or barber shops back then. The girls curled and styled their own hair, and spent a lot of time in front of the mirrors. When the boys' hair started looking a bit shaggy, and Dad's dose of Wild Root hair cream—or Mom's spit—wouldn't hold it together, Mom clipped the boys' hair, cutting it fairly short so she wouldn't have to do it again for a month or two. We called them butches.

The clipper whizzed and hair fell on the dish-drying towel Mom wrapped around our necks. It wasn't until we were older that we had the opportunity to go into town and get haircuts from a professional barber.

Lastly, large families usually found cheap entertainment on the weekends or nights once the chores were done. Many of us were content to challenge each other to a game of checkers or cards. We played board games like *Uncle Wiggly* or *Monopoly*; read books; gathered around the piano for sing-a-longs; played outdoors, taking turns on the tire swing; hunted and fished. You could count on one hand the times the entire family dined out in a year, not counting family reunions and potlucks.

The 4-H program taught my siblings about sewing, cooking, and growing vegetables. Once their 4-H projects were completed, they were taken to the county fair, where entries were judged and critiqued. Who didn't enjoy the aroma of cotton candy and caramel popcorn that filled the fair's night air? In one of the old schools located at the county fairgrounds, there were spelling contests or mathematic problems to solve on an old slate chalkboard. Children competed for pride and, of course, for a blue ribbon and bragging rights.

Even television served as entertainment relief, from the black and white era into the new color technology. We watched TV programs like *Bonanza, Wagon Train, The Roy Rogers Show*, the *Lawrence Welk* magical musical hour, TV news starring Walter Cronkite, or professional baseball or football games. If lucky, there was enough money to occasionally take the family to the movie theater, where grand musical productions such as *The Music Man*, and religious productions like *The Greatest Story Ever Told* and *The Ten Commandments* graced the screen.

On the Fourth of July, we'd travel to the county seat and watch fireworks from the roof of our aunt and uncle's house near the launch sites. Somehow, there were always a few firecrackers and cherry bombs to throw, plus bottle rockets to shoot.

When we could get away for a one-day trip, it was to visit tourist places such as Clear Lake, Iowa; Spillville, Iowa, where the Bily clocks were on display; a ball game at the former Metropolitan Stadium in Bloomington, Minnesota, to watch the Twins in action; the airport in Rochester, Minnesota, to watch the big passenger airplanes come in and take off; nearby state parks and lakes; the Amana Colonies in Iowa; more unique, but nearby, places.

We also found entertainment in our pets. There were always dogs on the farm, usually mixed breeds that made good rat and mice catchers when we shelled our mounds of corn. The dogs were also good with livestock, gathering in the cattle from the pasture or chasing off angry bulls. Most were friendly with guests, but their barks alerted us of anyone pulling into the driveway. Cats and kittens were always plentiful, somehow always gathering around the pie tin in the milk parlor while we were milking cows, eager to get a taste of some of the sweet, warm milk. Once in a great while, stray feral cats found their way into the barn. They were most unwelcome, as all they would do was hiss and run whenever they were approached. There was also the possibility they would spread rabies to pets, livestock, and people.

With all the busy work Mom endured week after week, her favorite release was writing letters to her siblings and a special friend. For about 50 years, she kept in contact with a pen pal from New Zealand, and the two shared stories about their lives and struggles in raising their families. They also exchanged gifts now and then during the holidays.

During her free time, Mom enjoyed listening to the radio for the local news and shared recipes programs, loved dancing waltzes and polkas at The Terp Ballroom in Austin, Minnesota, and was always ready to play a card game with family and friends. She still enjoys playing a good card game of *Sheephead, Five Hundred, Three Kings*, and *Bridge*, and has passed that love down to many of her children and grandchildren.

It didn't seem like money was the most important ingredient in keeping the morale of a large family in good spirits. Instead, the love shown by our parents always came shining through. They knew they were doing the best they could with what they had, in bringing up their children and creating memories that would last a lifetime.

Our family in the 1960s, back row from left, Frank, Sue, Chuck, Ruth and Al. Front row, Doris, Elaine, Mom Marcella, Mar, Dad Rudy, Marilyn and Ann.

Same family in 2018 when we celebrated Marcella's 90th birthday. Front from left, Sue, Mom Marcella and Elaine. In back, Mary, Chuck, Doris, Ruth, Frank, Marilyn, Ann and Al. Dad Rudy passed away in 1996.

What were some of your family chores?

Away

"I want to live here forever," my child said.

But that same child,

pounding the piano ivories,

or cuddling close for a story

will turn, look long

and then walk away.

Saying farewell to dreams of puffy

clouds of cotton candy, wondrous

dates, or coasting the hills

on bicycles and skates.

Ambitions of bigger-than-life

goals take over.

Time will never stand still again.

In passing, we'll hope we've touched their
heart,

be a refrigerator magnet to their

messages of needs. They'll come back,

pierce the silence, and fill the emptiness

that came once they left the nest.

Home will always be here,

almost as if the child has never left.

The adult world takes control,

but they'll always be our beautiful   children

and we'll be here, waiting for them.

A Child Again

Sometimes, on endless busy days,
I think of my life as a child.
Those days when the world's weight
was light as youth, carefree and wild.

I look upon my own children now
with no worries to tie them down
as they go through early life's trials
without hurt, or reason to frown.

For in their confines are enjoyments,
created by the simplest of pleasures.
No battles over the luxuries;
even the spoils are their treasures.

Responsibility is just a word to them.
Someday, when ready, they'll learn.
For now, being in the arms of loved ones
draws their utmost concern.

Their journey has just begun,
their travels will take them far.
What path they take is guided by
dreams once wished on a shooting star.

Their never-ending quest for knowledge,
their forever look of innocence,
bring loving thoughts of how, to a life,
children add great significance.

Chapter Nine

Bundle up

Winters in northern Iowa, a few miles from the Minnesota border, were what tall survival tales were made of, although most of those words held true. Winter was always a guest that overstayed its welcome, to most adults anyway. Not to children, though. A winter wonderland was a winter playground.

Ten to thirteen inches of snow at one time was a common occurrence where I lived in northern Iowa. Because of the heavy snowfall, farmers got on their tractors, hooked up their loader buckets, moved snow around their yards for at least two days, and piled it up high wherever a spot was available.

Those hills made for some wonderful sledding. Once we were finished going up and down those hills, it was on to other adventures. Each big mound had so many tunnels it resembled a big block of Swiss cheese.

Dad drove his Farmall H tractor with its loader attachment, as chains draped over the wheels jingled, to cut paths through the steep snow toward the dairy barn, around the chicken house, close to the hog house, around the garage, and right up to the steps of the family home. Those were places that had to be cleaned first so routine work on the farm could continue.

When all that was done, he allowed us to tie a rope or chain to the back of the tractor and he drove while the siblings took turns riding on an old tractor tire or a sled.

Winds whipped the snow for days, often keeping students home from school. Because our house was on a country gravel road, there were times it took a few days to get it plowed by the county. Some days we had to ride with Dad on the tractor to the nearest plowed blacktop, where the county plows first traveled. There were stop signs buried under drifts, and county snow-blowing trucks made paths ahead of vehicles so people could travel for emergency purposes.

Today's grocery stores are rushed and depleted whenever word gets out about an impending snowstorm, just like today. On our farm, food supplies were not a problem, as long as the chickens didn't go on strike, and the cows didn't turn up dry for their daily milking. There could be twenty inches of snow on the ground, but as long as chores weren't neglected, there was food on the dinner table.

At times a storm came up fast while we were still in school and early outs were inevitable. Or sometimes half the class couldn't make it in to school because of bad weather. Then, it was fun and games all day in our classrooms for those who were snowed in at school, like spelling bees or fun reading time, until our parents or neighbors could safely pick us up and take us home. Neighbors worked together to get the children home safe; our heads would be sticking out of the car windows at times, to let the driver know if he or she was blindly wandering too much toward the middle of the road, or heading for a ditch.

I chillingly recall blizzard days in the country, particularly at night when we snuggled under heavy blankets or worn quilts. All we had to do was look out our windows at our yard light and see the snow blowing straight across the dimly-lit area. We closed our eyes and listened in awe at the roar of the wind. When morning came and the smell of bacon and eggs drifted upstairs, it was our first indication that school was closed for the day. It meant Mom had time to cook a hearty breakfast before my brothers, sisters, and I had to go out into the cold and help scoop snow, do other chores, or just play.

Just as memorable was the day after the blizzards, when temperatures dipped well below zero and left the world looking like a frozen snow globe. Nothing started on its own, not the old pickup truck, the tractors, or the cars parked inside the garages. Even, to dad's discontent, his own sons had to be jump started.

Chores always went on as scheduled. We climbed a chute leading to the inside of the un-covered silo and scooped out the newly-fallen snow. Then we'd take a pickaxe and break up clumps of silage and throw it down the silage chute. From there the feed went into the barn, where the warmth from the cattle's bodies helped thaw the frozen feed and us.

The water in the cattle tank, thickened with ice, had to be melted away so the cattle could quench their thirst. A cast-iron heater, posi-tioned smack dab in the center of the tank, per-formed the melting task; it was fueled by chunks of coal that we bought from a local supplier. Black smoke, from coal that had been smothered with kerosene, rose through galva-nized, attached stovepipes and served as a sig-nal for the cattle to come and drink.

Heat lamps burned brightly throughout the frigid evening hours and kept the sows warm amidst their straw-filled pens in the far-rowing houses, staying on before, and after, their squeaky, grunting litters arrived.

We boiled water and poured it over frozen pipes in the hog house and chicken house. The next day the wind pushed snow to greater heights and shut down the rural countryside. Temperatures reached thirty below zero, or lower, and that didn't include wind chill readings.

We layered. We put on a double pair of gloves, three layers of jackets and coats over a shirt, sweatshirt and flannel shirt, two stocking hats, two pairs of socks, and five-buckle boots, and faced winter's wrath head on. It was a wonder we could even walk outside, but we had to. The animals depended on us.

The days that followed still had remnants of the blizzard. Piles of corn still on the cob that were stored outside, inside snow fencing, became mountains of snow. The winter storm left its calling card inside the uncovered buildings, too. Snow piled high on the hay bales stacked outside, the roofs of the sheds and barns, in the cattle yards, and the hog lots. The huge, long drifts blocked entries to fields and driveways, and any strong wind would blow it all shut again just hours after it was removed.

We came in from the winter cold after chores, shed our many layers, warmed up near the furnace, and sipped a cup of hot chocolate. These were warm memories of some very tough winters.

How did your family cope with the cold winters?

Snow Ballet

Each year about this time
when the weather turns to cold,
many wait with anticipation
for the snow ballet to unfold.

Winds from the north create the
eerie, howling sound,
moving along the autumn leaves
that gracefully whirl around.

And the bare tree branches appear
with their arms swaying to and fro;
the tone is set for the entrance of
the prima ballerina of the show.

Lightly, the dancing snow leaps onto
nature's stage.
Each step is hardly heard
but the action captivates the audience,
as both mystic and magic are stirred.

The snow twists and turns,
floating like feathers from the sky.
Soon the place is brightly decorated
with a white blanket piled high.

Once the orchestra music has faded and
the snow's graceful presence is felt,
what's left is just a lasting impression,
a memory too precious to melt.

Wintry Whining

Winter never exits routinely. The
slightest hint it's over is
only a mockery to wishful thinking
as the swirling snow clings
in piles at the doorstep.
Coldness fills a void for now, but it
is too raw, too tiresome, too brutal.
Time freezes, ice cold, in eerie stillness.
Yet life moves on, and we cringe,
knowing this is a place for penguins.
Now is not the time for faint-hearted ones.
Fight the grip it has. Don't let hope escape
or dip lower than the mercury
on the outside thermometer, which
snapped
after bitter punches from wintry blasts.
Yes, there is a time for all seasons,
but winter's welcome is worn.

It's like munching on a green apple,

so sour that it makes us pucker.

And only the milk of spring can settle the stomach.

Chapter Ten

Planting the Seeds

The garden is what saved my mother's children.

This was no ordinary farm garden that was plowed early in the year by my father, then disked over a couple of times so that the dirt was nice and loose. It was Dad's duty to plant the sweet corn with his tractor and corn planter on the far outside row of the garden.

The rest of the garden, about 180 feet long by about 90 feet wide, was Mom's turf, so to speak, and anyone who wanted to eat of the bounty from her turf had to find something to do in that garden.

I don't know how she had time to plan a garden, or even when she ordered the seeds, but this plot of ground was her outdoor entertainment, her way to relax. She'd take a day in the garden over a television soap opera any day of the week.

To her ten children it was rigorous work to dig those deep holes for the potatoes, to make straight rows for the radishes, to get all the proper spacing needed for the pea and string bean seeds, find spots for the cabbage and lettuce seeds, and make room for the pumpkins, watermelons, and squash.

There was a reason she involved all her children in gardening; the tasks kept most of them out of trouble. Idle minds and hands didn't happen too often on the farm, with chores and garden work always on the daily agenda. As the produce grew and blossomed, garden upkeep became even more important.

Most often, we'd be sent to the garden to pull weeds as our punishment for getting that bad grade on the report card, or for taunting another sibling. Woe to us for talking back, or fighting with our siblings, because garden duty was the ace up her sleeve in the hand that life dealt her.

We'd be ordered to till or hoe the garden in exchange for some misdoings. To Mom, walking the straight and narrow meant tilling the rows without wiping out a whole row of carrots. The disciplining may have continued through harvest, but the gathering of produce, and seeing the fruit of our labors, seemed satisfying.

We joined Mom in shucking the peas, husking the sweet corn, digging up potatoes, snapping the string beans, and more. Our reward was fresh produce on the supper table, and a fruitful harvest canned that lasted through the winter.

On canning day, the kitchen stove was covered with boiling kettles, and Mom was usually stirring the steaming pots. Once the canning jars were sterilized and filled, the dilled pickles, sweet corn, and beans were placed in the basement pantry. It was a blessing to have vegetables in the winter months to fill out the dinner table. At a time when video games were coming into their own, when television was entertainment and not obsession, and when life seemed much simpler, a garden was a colorful haven, and a mother's pride and joy. Colorful flowers like peonies enriched the garden's borders, particularly around Mother's Day.

Mom felt that if she weeded out the bad influences, her children would turn out okay, too.

There's nothing wrong with that philosophy, even today.

Did your family have a garden and what did you grow?

Farmer's Request

As I am ready to leave this earth,
my family, and friends this day,
Lord, can you lead me
to a special place along the way.

Guide me to this place I love,
please let my spirit once more roam.
Though I left it and moved elsewhere,
I have dear memories for this land called
Home.

You see Lord, I was a farmer
and was darn proud of the life I led.
From sunrise to darkness I worked hard,
often taking my worries to bed.

See Lord, you have to understand
why I chose this profession.
You only need to know that
working the land was my greatest
obsession.

There's something about farming,
and I hope this doesn't sound too odd.
But the most pleasant memories I have
would be hitching the horses to plow the
sod.

To plant acres of corn
and spend time to walk each row.
There's nothing better for a farmer's heart
than watching a healthy crop grow.

You can awaken to a glorious sunrise
or watch the wind make the oats sway,
or catch the smell after a fresh spring rain
or the scent of newly-cut hay.

You learned to appreciate the solitude
and peaceful times when doing the
livestock chores, and learning to have a
little fun even if it's just cleaning livestock
floors.

There's just that sense of accomplishment,
which I'm sure, Lord, you will agree
when my wife and children
appreciate farming, just like me.

I loved the earth and nature.
Those feelings still remain.
My grateful thanks to you, Lord,
for the fruitful rewards I gained.

Now we should move onward, Lord,
and if it's by Your will,
I'll gladly be of service if
some of heaven's acres need to be tilled.

(Author Unknown)

Chapter Eleven

School and Sack Lunches

I see it in my mind over and over again: opening my brown lunch bag in the corner of a classroom and feasting my eyes on some homemade bread that was toasted and sprinkled with sugar and cinnamon. That was heaven back then; still is now.

Sometimes Mom would throw in a sandwich, a small piece of beef left over from the previous night's big meal, or a fried egg sandwich on toast. There might even be a banana in the lunch bag.

Once kindergarten was in the rearview mirror, it was time to take that step toward elementary school. All of my siblings had the opportunity to complete the full eight grades at a small Catholic school in Stacyville.

At one time the school held classes for up to twelve grades. The high school eventually had a different name than Visitation School, called Marian High School. The high school closed after the 1967-1968 school year, and those going beyond eighth grade at Visitation enrolled in surrounding public schools, many to St. Ansgar High School. Elementary grades at Visitation were on the first and basement floors of the parochial school, while the high school area consisted of all of the upper floor and the classroom sections in the lunchroom-gymnasium addition to the school.

During those first eight grades at Visitation School, transportation to and from school were the responsibilities of the parents. That meant driving in all sorts of weather conditions, such as blizzards, on gravel and blacktop roads, through drifts that sometimes were higher than the vehicle. When spring rains and warmth arrived, defensive driving was required to weave through the frost boils and mud that stalled many a car or wrecked many an axle. If traveling by car was not negotiable on the gravel roads, parents would get out the tractor and a hayrack and transport their children, and neighboring kids, to the more passable, hard-top roads.

There were several consecutive years that our family had from three to five siblings going to the same school in different grades at the same time.

First grade was unique. This is where I met my classmates for life. My class was a large one, with more than twenty students. Considering the town of Stacyville had less than 500 people at the time, this class size was quite significant. One special feature of our classroom was a huge coat closet that had hooks to hold our winter wraps and boots. In northern Iowa, winters stretched long—from late November to early April and beyond—a lengthy time to be wearing jackets and coats to school, and for constant outdoor recesses. Smells of wet jackets and rubber boots wafted from the closet into the classroom, where it blended with the familiar odor of hot radiator pipes that spewed welcome heat on a chilly day. If the mittens we wore got wet, they would find a spot on the radiators and all were dry before the class bell rang, signaling the end of the school day.

The huge, black chalkboard stretched across the front of the room. Above it was a wide chart displaying the capital and small letters of the alphabet, useful when learning to spell small words like cat and dog, or when using the words in sentences. Each day started with a school mass, a classroom prayer, and a recitation of the Pledge of Allegiance, our hands firmly placed on our hearts.

"See Jane run. See Spot (the dog) run. See Puff (the cat) go. Run, Puff, run! Run, Spot, run!" That was from our *Dick and Jane* reading book that motivated us to find more children's books from the school's library or the classroom's bookshelves, complete with colorful illustrations.

Second grade, held in the lower floor of the school, was a special year of faith as we rehearsed for First Communion and First Confession. On that day of receiving our First Communion, during a special Mass, the girls wore lacy communion dresses and veils while the boys dressed in white shirts, black bow ties or long ties, and our Sunday-best pants. In preparation, we memorized prayers and liturgical procedures, so that once we received our white candle, a special black prayer book, a rosary, and a scapula, we would know the meaning of each part of the Mass.

Our parents' reward was a large photograph of our First Communion class, plus a picture and news article in the local newspaper about the event. Our reward from our parents was a nice gift, as a memento of the celebration, plus a homemade cake of our very own to share with the family, emphasizing the significance of the occasion.

As we progressed in school, we celebrated the sacrament of Confirmation, which was a pretty big affair because we had to, in homage, kiss the ring of the Bishop when he arrived to officiate at the ceremony. We answered tough questions from the Bishop and, once the church ceremony was complete and we were moved by the Spirit (I kept listening for the sound of blowing wind), we were entitled to add another saint's name to go with our middle name. Much thought went into the selection and my choice was Saint Francis because, well, he and animals had a way with each other, and being a farmer's son, I guess I did, too.

We also had to have a Confirmation sponsor and mine was my Dad's best friend, a tall, lanky farmer who had helped with some electrical wiring, installing several fuse boxes and silo unloaders, on our family farm. On the night of Confirmation rehearsal, he and Dad took me into one of Stacyville's taverns (other stores were closed at night) and my sponsor bought me the sweetest, largest, tastiest taffy bar I ever had the privilege of chewing.

The middle grades are a blur for me, maybe because of all the good behavior I had to exhibit while in the classroom. There was a good reason for that: when you're one of a big family attending a smaller school, there were times when an older or younger sibling shared the same classroom, with the same teacher, even though the brother or sister was in a higher or lower grade level.

In most cases, what happened in school almost NEVER stayed in school. Parents most often had an inside source who would tell if there were scoldings or conversations from teachers about inappropriate acts, missed assignments, or bad grades. I definitely had to keep the halo straight and tall.

Our morning snacks were usually carried in brown bags or prized lunch pails. Some of the lunch pails I had featured characters from TV shows like *The Lone Ranger* or *Roy Rogers.* I still savor the taste of egg sandwiches or cinnamon and sugar toast on homemade bread, both packed by Mom. The snack usually tided me over until the noon meal. Lunch was served up by Rose Huemann and Gertie Metz, legendary highly-experienced cooks, and other volunteers as the classes went in shifts to get their lunch tickets punched, so they could quickly consume their meals and then head out for recess.

Most of the teachers serving the school were nuns from the Franciscan Order within the Dubuque, Iowa, diocese. Sister Lila, Sister Nora, Sister Jeremy, and Sister Edith are several who come to my mind during my years at the elementary school. Others pointed out to me by siblings and friends included Sister William, Sister Ronald, Sister Nicholas, Sister Bridget, Sister Theophil, Sister Olivia, Sister Liam, Sister Roger, Sister Cora, Sister Mary, Sister Irma, Sister Marlys, Sister Bona Joan, Sister Julita, Sister Marian, Sister Loren, Sister Noel, Sister Howard, Sister Gabriel, Sister Bosco and Sister Anchilla.

Other full-time teachers included residents from the community. Mrs. Margaret Brown was my third and fourth grade teacher; she also instructed several of my older and younger siblings. I recall a vivid, emotional day in her classroom, when it was announced that John F. Kennedy, our nation's president, was shot in Dallas. Mrs. Brown couldn't speak as we worked our problems on the blackboard. It was a very sad day.

My favorite highlight in junior high was our physical education instructor, Dick Hogan, and his intraschool basketball league. He was also the head boys' high school basketball coach at our small school, so when we were in the elementary grades, he got a glimpse of the athletic talent coming up the chute.

Many of our classmates eagerly anticipated Mr. Hogan's weekly posting of the blue eight-by-ten paper on the junior high classroom blackboard that detailed, in perfect handwriting, the previous week's player scoring, game scores, and the school league standings.

Considering how clumsy I was, I was usually listed at the very bottom of the scoring list. My only basketball field goal on that coveted list was a lucky half-court shot I made during a school league game. It bounced high on the rim about three times and fell through the net, forcing the game into overtime. We ended up losing the game, but that loss was forgotten in my moment of glory.

More lay teachers remembered by my siblings and friends included Mrs. Germaine

Blake, Bill Morgan, Melvin Reding, Mr. and Mrs. Baldus, Mr. Indra, Mrs. Margaret Heimer, Ms. Natvig, Mr. Anderson, Mr. Wellendorf, Ms. Denzel, Ms. Fitzpatrick, Mrs. Angela May, Mrs. Schotanous, Mrs. Heimerman, Mrs. Stibal and Mrs. Klassen. Walt Durbin, at the time, served as janitor.

School playground equipment, like the swings and sliver-inducing see-saws, saw their share of use throughout the school year by elementary students. The squeaking sound of the rocker swing, a wooden one that could hold up to eight or more students, still stands out in the minds of those who attended Visitation School because it competed against the screams of the children. There were quick ball games to play and several snow hills to conquer, usually playing King of the Hill, plus numerous tunnels dug in the frozen mounds.

It wasn't all 'hitting the books hard' in the classroom, either. Teachers broke up some of the structured monotony with impromptu spelling bees, stretching exercises, sessions listening to fun songs like "Tiny Bubbles" while dancing hula style, speech contests, ten minute 'mind breaks' where we put our heads on our desks, plus field trips to the countryside or to movie theaters, to see school-related movies like *The Ten Commandments* or *The Greatest Story Ever Told*.

We were able to attend high school plays and sports events, watching the Marian Mustangs and the Visitation V-Hawks in action. School picnics at the end of the school year were also part of the fun. They were usually held near a rural pasture's creek, where students could wade in the water or enjoy a fire-roasted hotdog or two cooked up by parents or volunteers.

Each year there was a school carnival, when students could earn some prizes or feast on popcorn balls; an afternoon off from the rigors of worksheets, tests, and homework. The most popular booth was the fish pond, where students tossed a line over a partition, felt a tug on the string, pulled it back up, and found a prize clipped by a clothespin at the end of the string.

The boys had to study a different language, but not in a classroom setting. Latin had to be memorized so they could become Mass servers, particularly during the church services when all responses had to be answered in Latin. Students reaching the age of Mass servers had laminated scripts available that they would study outside of the classroom, sometimes on the school entrance steps, before presenting themselves as Mass server candidates.

In the spring of 1968 an announcement was made that the parochial high school attached to the grade school would be closed.

The grade school eventually closed its doors, too, and in 2012 the school building was razed, leaving only the gymnasium and cafeteria for community and parish events.

There are memories and artifacts my family and I have accumulated, helping rekindle memories of those years at Visitation School.

Memorable sounds included the boiler kicking in and the whistling of the radiators; chalk squeaking on the blackboard in the hands of teacher or student; children's laughter and chatter in the hallways and coming in from recess; the clicking of the slide projectors; the pots and pans clanging in the school kitchen; the reassuring, kind voices of the teachers; the ringing of the bells during the church service; hearing someone reading aloud from a book; scoldings for inappropriate behavior; pencil sharpeners continually whittling down students' No. 2 pencils for the Basic Skills Tests, because remember you had to keep the marks within the small circles on the answer pages.

Sights included the newly-cleaned classrooms, completed by the school's janitor, Walt Durbin, and others who helped prep the school each day; the Franciscan Sisters and lay teachers who engaged the students' imaginations through instruction, play, and prayer; the flags flapping in the wind on the flagpole in front of the school; frustration, disappointment, and triumph on students' faces after competing in math or spelling competitions; large maps that showed us our country and the world; television programs shown during classes about Iowa and its early Native American inhabitants and culture.

Smells included the odor of fresh air [farm smells] lingering on students coming in from recess; a whiff of the sawdust compound used to clean up messes from sick children (I always pitied the poor janitor or teacher who had the task of cleaning up the mess.); whatever was cooking in the ovens of the school's kitchen; the mustiness of a closet filled with wet coats and mittens; hot steam as it escaped from the hot, metal radiators; art projects involving markers, crayons, or glue; incense burning during a Holy Day church service; science experiments gone awry.

All in all, those eight years at Visitation School were important in establishing a good foundation for all of us siblings, not only for the next four years of high school, but also in life.

What do you remember about elementary and junior high school, and who were some of your teachers?

Nothin'

The young girl's weary eyes clash with her
mom's glances

after the elementary school empties.

"What did you do today?" Mom asks.

"Nothin'," barks the child.

"Except there's a new kid in class. And at

recess I fell. Scraped a knee. It bled.

I didn't cry, though. We played 'boys chase
girls'

in gym class today. I let them catch me.

"Art teacher wants money for new colors.

Librarian says I lost a book. Teacher said

I have perfect writing, but my spelling is
bad.

Nurse said there's head lice going around.

"Oh, I got a detention, but it wasn't my fault,

and I lost all my pens and pencils.

The cap for my glue popped off and my desk is sticky.

Fell asleep during math."

When Dad comes home, he asks the child:

"Anything happen at school?"

A blank stare from the child, then the standard answer:

"Nothin'."

Chapter Twelve

Music Programs

While at Stacyville Visitation School, it was customary to have a Christmas program in December for both the elementary and upper level grades.

One of those years, the high school basketball team had a very successful season, and along with that was the Christmas program that my family and I attended. I had gone to a couple of basketball games at the high school and noticed the sharpshooters and the skinny, tall players who were also involved in the music program. When it was time for a solo, I couldn't believe they picked the team's tall center to perform it. As he voiced the words to "Birthday of a King," I was amazed at his singing voice and perfect pitch; he normally called out the defenses and offenses and hauled down the rebounds during the games on the court.

It left a lasting impression.

Music has always been a part of our family as long as I can remember. Many of my patience-minded siblings took piano lessons; some participated in high school choirs and still sing in church choirs. Piano wasn't the sole instrument floating around the homestead, although it was a main gathering point when it was time for a sing-a-long or recital rehearsing. Some siblings played band instruments like the drums and clarinet; others passed around an accordion and harmonica. There was also a violin that, unfortunately, met its match trying to win me over as its prize pupil. That never happened, although I regret it to this day.

Music lessons were taught by nuns of the parish and usually required a trip to the convent. At the time, I might have been the only boy in my class that was excused to have violin lessons. But, I didn't want to be labeled a sissy, so wanted nothing to do with it. After a month or so of the lessons, a moment of frustration came during a home practice session; I put the violin down and absentmindedly sat on it, destroying the strings and the instrument's bridge that held those strings together. It was one of my few true regrets, because I'd love to be able to play the violin today.

My mom made sure all of her children had opportunities to play musical instruments. Our parents continued to offer encouragement about music as long as the child persevered, got better, and didn't complain. I enjoyed singing, although I kept that enjoyment under a bushel basket. Some of the song lyrics we sang at school recitals still stick with me. Here are a few of them that linger from those elementary years.

Roll On

At night when the cattle are sleeping/on a saddle I pillow my head/and up at the stars I lie peeping/from out of my soft grassy bed.

How often and often I wondered/at night when lying alone/if every bright star up in heaven/is a big people's world like our own.

Roll on, roll on, roll on little doggie's roll on, roll on/Roll on, roll on, roll on little doggies, roll on.

Railroad Tracks

Stay away from the railroad tracks/it isn't a place to play/for trains go fast when they go past/and you may be in the way.

Ice skating

Ice skating is nice skating but here's some advice about ice skating/Never skate where the ice is thin/or the ice will break and you'll fall right in/and come up with icicles under your chin…if you skate where the ice is thin.

Whole World in His Hands

He's got the whole world in his hands/He's got the whole wide world, in his hands/He's got the whole world (you and me brother/sister, little bitty baby or whatever you'd like to substitute here) in his hands/He's got the whole world in His hands.

Kookaburra

Kookaburra sings in the old gum tree/Merry, merry king of the bush is he/Laugh, Kookaburra laugh, kookaburra/Gay your life must be.

Rain Drops

I saw rain drops on my window/Joy is like the rain/Bit by bit the river grows/til all it once it overflows/Joy is like the rain.

Autumn Winds

Blow, autumn winds, blow/Shake gold from the tree/When the school work is done there is football and fun/Blow, autumn winds, blow.

I can't leave this chapter of Visitation School without some insight into its music programs. Every student had to attend music class and all had to sing in the choirs, even if they couldn't hit a pitch, hadn't the slightest idea of what constituted a quarter note or a whole note, or couldn't keep up with the beat no matter how the pendulum would swing on the music teacher's metronome as it ticked away on top of the piano.

The Christmas concerts were probably the most fun, and more enticing if you got to be on stage as part of the live Nativity scene. It was also nice that we skipped a class or two to rehearse the program as the days before the concert grew shorter. That meant less time spent on classroom subjects like math and geography, which was fine with me.

There were times we had to be part of the choral groups and were also assigned to dress as angels, sometimes posing on ladders sporting glitter-laced wings and halos made of pipe cleaners, as we surrounded the crib scene. Shepherds wore colored sheets or towels around their shoulders and were armed with staffs. However, the prestigious roles went to whoever was selected by the teachers to play the roles of Mary and Joseph.

Singing was a student requirement for Catholic Church services, the regular daily morning Mass and, more often than not, one of us would get a small scolding from the religious teachers for fooling around or talking when all attention should have been on the service responses and music. The pipe organ in the choir loft accompanied all voices, with the lyrics of the songs sometimes in Latin.

A spontaneous song then, likened to the two recesses a day and the physical education classes, helped break the monotony of a long day of worksheets, reading lessons, addition and subtraction, spelling, geography, science, and social studies.

Music taught us to stand before an audience and perform without fright, and to conquer our doldrums on a dreary day by dancing in the classroom aisles and swaying to Hawaiian ukuleles. During special classes, we also got the chance to refine our comprehension and appreciation of the great tale of *Peter and the Wolf* as the engrossing storyline and instrumental interpretation poured through the speakers of the school's old, but dependable, record player.

It was likely during these earlier years that a senior high soloist, singing that glorious solo in the warm gymnasium on a cold December night, got his or her first taste, and undoubtedly not the last, of what music and the arts could add to the soul and spirit, while performing on that grand stage that we call life.

Was there a special activity in school that you always enjoyed?

Chapter
Thirteen
School's Last Day

What child didn't enjoy that last day of school? Recesses were longer and teachers were more forgiving and, for some reason, seemed to be smiling a lot more as the school year wound down.

It was the day we received our colorful green or blue report cards to present to our parents, and on the back of that card, it would tell us if our marks—from A to F—were good enough to advance us into the next elementary grade level or on into high school. There were probably times that we just squeaked by, so there was always that tension on the last school day as we hoped we weren't on the bubble.

That last day of school we cleaned our desks and brought home the broken colors, the half bottle of glue, pencils without lead or chewed easers, old worksheets that should have gone home months before, and whatever else had found its way into the dark hollows and deepest recesses of our domain. We ripped the paper-grocery-sack covers filled with doodling off our textbooks. The teachers supplied us with sandpaper and, with the book tightly closed, we sat at our desks and sanded all the pages. The books' covers might have looked worn after years of use, but the pages appeared nice and bright for the students using those texts next year.

Some students cleaned chalkboard erasers, an outside job for sure. Clapping the chalkboard erasers together always resulted in a cloud of chalk dust that you breathed in and got all over your clothes. The task wasn't finished until the erasers were completely restored to their true color, usually black or green.

There was one final church service, and with the final blessing from the parish priest, school was officially over and report cards were distributed. And Hallelujah! Summer vacation began. Of course, the newness of the summer break rubbed off quickly as parents began delegating summer chores. There were still household and farm chores to finish, first and second crops of hay to bale, weeds to pull in the garden, lawns to mow, eggs to gather; there were very few vacations from our chores.

But it was also the time of year to sign up for summer activities. That meant swimming lessons for all of the siblings, taught at a public pool in Osage or St. Ansgar, about twelve miles either way from our farm. Most of my siblings were adept at swimming, thanks to these lessons, but to someone like me with a body that tended to sink like a boulder, learning to swim was not in the cards. First came the stage of learning to bob your head into the water, holding your breath underwater with your eyes open, then floating on your back, then kicking and, eventually, if you got that far, using your hands and feet to swim the length of the pool.

The fears that led to me not gaining full swim certification were not of drowning. I was too self-conscious, I guess, of wearing swim trunks that bloated every time I stepped into the deeper water. As a farm lad, I was more accustomed to constantly wearing full-length blue jeans; my pale legs probably blinded the swim instructor and the surrounding students.

I didn't like the cold showers we took before getting into the pool and after the lessons. Unfortunately, the pool was never warm because our lessons were usually early in the morning before the sun had a chance to warm it. And no matter how hard I tried, I couldn't swim a lick. When I inhaled water, it added to my weight, and I'd sink to the bottom of the pool. Fortunately, I was rescued by the instructor who simply smiled and said, "Nice try."

However, I didn't avoid all water. I enjoyed joining my brothers and sisters as we waded in the creek that wound through our farm acreage to catch tadpoles, or raced through the garden sprinklers on a hot, steamy day. It was even more relaxing as we rushed through mud puddles, although that wasn't something Mom appreciated. It's just that mud squishing through bare toes was very exhilarating and way better than swimming in the cows' water tank, which was shared by small bullheads unfit to eat that could poke you with their sharp fins.

On rainy days there were plenty of board games to keep us busy inside, like Life and Dominoes, plus card games and playing pranks on siblings.

My brothers and I pranked our sisters often. One memorable laugher was a radio bulletin we concocted in our upstairs bedroom one night after chores. One of my brothers had a walkie-talkie set, which was the main prop in this trickery. At the time, my parents were away, so we were in charge of the babysitting.

We secretly hid one of the walkie-talkies behind a radio. My brothers went downstairs and told the girls that there was a bulletin from the radio station. He turned on the walkie-talkie and I, in my most news-casting voice, issued an all-points emergency about a truck carrying lions and bears that had overturned several miles from the KGLO television tower, which was about three miles from our home. Wild animals were on the loose! That news really startled the girls.

When the second announcement came that the animals were moving closer and closer to our home, they were in panic mode. We finally let the cat out of the bag, telling them it was only a prank; there were many jittery nerves to calm that night and some reprimanding words the next day from Mom and Dad.

My most anticipated summer activity occurred when the local newspaper announced the sign-up for the town's summer youth baseball program. The age divisions included Pee Wees and Midgets. There also was a Wee Wees program, too, for the really young players. Baseball, above all sports, was my favorite pastime.

Because we lived in the country, six miles or so from town, my only means of transportation to practices and games was pedal power. After all, my parents didn't have time to break away from working the farm, doing laundry, or other household chores while raising ten children. The rule was that if I wanted to play organized youth baseball, I also had to have an organized means of transportation.

Since Dad couldn't spare his tractor for an hour or two on three or four days a week, I faithfully strapped my baseball mitt on the bicycle's handlebars and pedaled my way into town.

A neighbor friend joined me in the summer program; he had even further to pedal than my jaunt on gravel and blacktop roads. The baseball program was funded by its registration fees and the city we represented, drawing participants from both city and rural families.

There were no such things as ten-speed, or even five-speed, bicycles in our neck of the woods at that time. Our family had typical 'bargain garage sale' bicycles with dented front fenders and drooping chains. The balloon-tired two-wheeler I rode had only one speed, which was as fast as I could pedal it. If there was a hill to climb, I relied on my muscles, not on the downshifting of gears.

There were times when fast wasn't quick enough because dogs from farms along our route would wait at the end of their driveways for an opportunity to nip at our heels. We always hoped that the farmers were in their fields with the dogs, and that we would have a brief respite from their fangs. At the end of practices, or returning home from games, I knew that I'd have to run that same gauntlet again and face those same dogs, who would be waiting for me as if they had my schedule firmly implanted in their minds.

I always thought country boys had a slight advantage over any others when it came to baseball. Country lads were known for frequently picking up rocks and sticks and swatting the rocks over fences. They relished playing baseball games with other lads and gals in neighboring yards and fields.

Coaches knew that many country lads also had power. Those haybale luggers, milk can haulers, and rock pickers had built up muscles doing daily chores and could usually throw well or smash the baseball. So, country lads, as well as city boys, could play the sport equally well.

I recall, after the evening milking chores, when my Dad would get out this old, round, ugly catcher's mitt that looked like it had been left out in the rain too long. He'd scavenge through the garage and pull out a small board, which he'd put in front of him for home plate and say, "Pitch to me."

We'd throw that baseball until it got dark, with him calling out balls and strokes. This was the same man that got up at five a.m. every day, working hard all day long raising crops and tending to livestock. He still made time at sunset to play some catch with his oldest son, and that was one of our good times together.

The city program provided the bats and balls and we furnished our own mitts, but it was always nice to have our own baseball equipment. We balanced it on our arms while we coasted on our bicycles, sometimes with no hands on the handlebars. Somehow, I think the coaches, usually members of the high school baseball squad, preferred us using our own wooden bats so that it was us, and not the city, that was at a loss when the bat cracked because the hitter had the bat's trademark facing the wrong way.

Teams carpooled to towns of similar size for league play, including the Iowa towns of Riceville, Alta Vista, Elma, Osage, St. Ansgar, Cresco, and more. Elma and Osage had rather unique ballparks that featured whitewashed outfield walls. Ball diamonds with grandstand seating were a real luxury in my day.

I never worried about cutting my arm on chain-link fences. I was more worried about breaking through a weak board, going after a fly ball. Many of the ball diamonds were on fairground property, and sometimes we were part of the county fair's entertainment.

Our home baseball field in Stacyville had windbreak, or corn cribbing, fencing that wasn't as high as other baseball venues. The right field fence wasn't as far from home plate, which intrigued left-hand pull-hitters, who always seemed to be swinging for the fences.

The Pee Wees played on game day first, followed by the Midgets. When one team played, the other team got to flood the concession stand and load up on sweets, popcorn, a hot dog, and a soda, purchased with a small allowance afforded to us from our parents. After the games, the results of the league contests were printed in the weekly newspaper, *The Monitor Review*, a newspaper I would later work for. It was fun reading the accounts of those games and seeing your name in print.

Even when I had to wear a baseball uniform that was twice my size, and had a sponsor's name on the back of it that hadn't been in business for many years, I enjoyed the thrill of competition, the fastball coming over the center of the plate, and the sound of the ball hitting the sweet spot on the bat.

Also, during the summer, we'd anxiously await our summer *Weekly Reader* and *Boys Life* publications that were filled with stories, puzzles, and games. My siblings and I would wait by the edge of the driveway, looking for that cloud of gravel dust kicked up by the tires of the mailman as he made his rural rounds. Once he got to our mailbox, he'd reach out his window and hand us the letters or magazines, and then reach over his seat and present us each with a candy treat.

Other summer vacation ventures included trips to aunts' and uncles' homes for family reunions, picnics in the park, visits to the county fair, trips to nearby tourist attractions, going to drive-in movies, watching Fourth of July fire-works, and enjoying the waters of Clear Lake and other surrounding lakes. We also indulged in a trip to the former Metropolitan Stadium in Bloomington, Minnesota, to take part in the annual Knot Hole Minnesota Twins game and professional player clinic sponsored for the youth each summer by a local fraternal youth organization. Good times.

The creek running through our farm was a blessing to me and my siblings. We enjoyed splashing our feet and catching the tadpoles that congregated along the bank's lush, tall grass and, if we were really lucky, we'd find a turtle.

Some days we'd hang an ordinary garden hose, attached to a nearby hydrant, across the clothesline and run back and forth under the cold running water, with no care in the world about any type of water bill.

During hay baling time, we'd take long water breaks, gulping down ice cold water or lemonade while we cooled off in the shade of a hayrack in the open field. Once in a while, Mom would throw in some rhubarb dessert or cookies, to keep us going strong, load after load.

At milking time, through the dog days of summer, we'd open doors and get as much air movement as possible inside the inferno we called the barn. We'd welcome any signs of clouds on the horizon, which meant a cold front was on the way and cool breezes would soon sweep through the barn, drying the sweating cows and keeping their tails from whacking at the flies landing on their backs. It was no fun milking hot, sweaty, restless cows in the humid Iowa heat.

In the hog barn, we'd spray down the panting sows, who just wanted to find a puddle of mud and plop into it for the rest of the day. We made sure that all of our livestock, and the family pets, had plenty of water to get them through the scorching summer temperatures.

Inside the house, it could also be unbearably hot. The screen doors and electric fans were all we had until years later when window air conditioner units were installed. Just as it was in the winter when the siblings would hog all the heating vents, the same was true of the siblings, standing for countless minutes in front of the fans on the tables and countertops, hogging all the air movement.

When it was time to sleep, we put our pillows next to an open window, sniffing for any breeze stirring through the trees and around the house. We would fall asleep to the wind rustling through the nearby cornfields, the chirping of crickets, and cows mooing in the distance; anything to help take our minds off of the heat.

If we didn't get enough sleep at night, there was nothing better than to break away from our chores that next day, find a big shade tree, lean against the trunk, and catch a few winks before anybody knew we were missing. It was pure pleasure, as long as you didn't oversleep and let the water in the cow tank overflow, or neglect some other important chore.

It was almost as pleasant as going on a Sunday drive to the nearest drive-in restaurant and ordering a root beer float or a tall ice cream cone. Nothing was wrong with that, especially when the special of the day was two scoops of vanilla or chocolate ice cream. Just thinking of biting into that cone, or a frozen juice bar, still makes me shiver.

Once the corn stalks are tall, lean, and yellow, the country pace quickens as harvesting begins. That's when the reality of another school year strikes, heralding the rush of bargain clothes shopping, including finding that elusive husky size. School supplies are assembled for distribution on the kitchen table. The second cutting of hay is in the barn, the oats are combined, straw bales are moved to the cattle and hog pens, leaves start turning colors, and the blistering temperatures begin to cool.

The brothers and sisters are abuzz with conversations about who their new teacher will be, and what awaits them in the classroom, all gearing up for that first day of school. It's a day of giddy anticipation, with new aspirations, possible new friendships, and fanciful wonderings about what's to come.

Summer vacation fades into a blurry past and our big family focuses somewhat nervously on what lies ahead, closing the book on another summer, having gained a few more months of maturity. We open up a chapter on new beginnings and start the school year with a clean slate.

There's no looking back now as we are introduced to new memories that will fill dozens of school yearbooks to come.

Where did you go for your summer vacations?

Fall Fashion Show

Welcome all,
take a look and see
the beautiful color
that robes this tree.

Splendor of leaves, visible in
bright yellow or rusty red.
But one quick warning:
the coat of leaves will soon shed.

For dressing up a
bare piece of ground,
bundled cornstalks are
the most popular we've found.

Accessories include pumpkins,
large and small,
that decorate all the stalk stacks,
short or tall.

Milkweed pods,
and the white furs they wear.
Materials include fluffy seeds
eager to take to the air.

A garden all decked out
in tangled brown vines,
potato hills dug up in rows
of almost straight lines.

A perfume to consider
for your free taking,
is the sweet aroma of pumpkin pie
as it is in the oven baking.

A perfectly round gem that
all will be noticing soon
is the magnificent appearance
of the glorious harvest moon.

So, it appears Mother Nature
certainly knows
how to put on the best
of all the fall fashion shows.

Chapter
Fourteen
Intimidation

Here I was, a ninth-grade high school student, blindfolded at the Freshman Initiation Dance, attempting to use a funnel to feed food morsels into another freshman student's mouth, in front of a high school audience full of upper classmen. The entire freshman class all had some embarrassing task to perform, as decided by the senior high leadership. The intimidation level was high during those early weeks of high school. As a matter of fact, the whole freshman year was rather daunting, to say the least.

There were so many unknowns. How would the integration of schools work out once our parochial high school closed? What strangers would come into our lives? What activities would be available? Would classroom subjects be difficult?

Would I miss the bus?

I usually made the bus, but there were some close calls. One morning I decided, on my 100-yard dash to the bus that was waiting for me at the end of our farm drive, I would slide across ice that had formed in a ditch near the driveway. But, in my haste, I never checked to see if that ice was solid.

It wasn't. To my horror and embarrassment, I broke through the ice. The water was about knee deep; my school clothes were soaked and my homework assignments were drowned. The bus driver, seeing my plight, ordered me to go back inside and change into dry clothes. He would wait for me.

I got back on the bus a bit red faced, but at least free from catching my death of cold, and very grateful for a patient bus driver. Unfortunately, when my high school teachers were told what happened to my homework, they were less forgiving.

Our school district covered plenty of rural territory and included mainly the towns of Mona, Meyer, Stacyville, Grafton, Carpenter, Toeterville, Otranto and St. Ansgar, which was the site of the district's high school that all my siblings graduated from. A multitude of busses traveled the rural hardtops, gravel roads, and highways, bringing kids who had no driver's licenses, while other students arrived in their own modes of transportation. Bus pick up times were early or late, depending on where you lived on the route. My two older sisters attended the same school I did, at the same time, and our bus driver usually showed up early enough so we had to quickly down our cinnamon-and-sugar toast breakfast and rush to the end of the driveway where the red lights were flashing on the bus.

My first inclination would be to find an empty seat behind the bus driver. I knew he would be too focused on driving and unable to carry on a conversation. That was fine with me because I wasn't much of a talker myself. The back of the bus was always filled first and alive with conversation.

High school was indeed an adjustment when I found my freshman class enrollment was more than 100 students. That in itself was a factor in creating some uneasiness, especially because the eighth-grade class at our parochial school had under 25 students.

There was a big assembly on the first day of high school in the gymnasium, where we met all the new classmates who would be a part of our lives for the next four years. It was also the advent of modular scheduling. Each module consisted of twenty minutes, so an hour-long, large-group class would stretch over three modules. Large group classes had all the freshmen in one room, where teachers lectured with microphones or gave out class tests. I felt safe in these large settings because I was less likely to be called on for answers. But during these large group meetings, more tests were administered and more pop quizzes were given, much to the chagrin of students who didn't review their lessons the previous night, or neglected all their homework assignments.

Small group classes usually lasted two modules or less. Our teachers seemed more relaxed in these settings, joking with students and offering help on subjects, some not related to textbooks.

All of us were assigned to homerooms, where we gathered at the start and end of each day. We were bound to the same homeroom until the day we graduated. My homeroom was the high school's Future Farmers of America (FFA) and shop classroom, which would have been more comfortable had I been more involved in those classes.

Each homeroom seemed to have its cast of characters. There were those who excelled in the classroom and rarely strayed from honor roll qualifications. Others acted like they didn't want to be in school because there were more important quests to conquer, like helping with the harvest or planting in the spring. A few were there to socialize and be class clowns. Then there was me, who didn't really fit in too well, and instead just went with the flow.

I was involved in shop only a little, learning a couple of skills in woodworking and metals like replacing loose boards on fences and shingling a roof.

Alas, my Dad's talents of invention and creativity never rubbed off on me; my shop projects always appeared more destructive than constructive. Wood projects were usually not squared or planed correctly, and were highly rough or uneven. I tried to make a step stool for my mom, but the legs wobbled so much that it was considered unsafe to use.

When a rumor went around that someone used the power planer wrong and the wood flew from the machine and put a hole in the shop wall, probably half the woodworking class thought that person was me. It wasn't, at least not that time.

The box I made in metals class was likely too dangerous to use because of its sharp edges and loose welds. I got by on my grades, but the instructors likely shaped their final grade decisions on resigned effort rather than visual merit.

My two younger brothers, however, were more gifted in all the shop classes. They learned to use my dad's welder at home so their shop class projects stayed together well and had a better chance of survival than mine.

There were several vocational programs in high school that captured the varied interests of many boys and girls, from welding to FFA. As much as I loved living on the farm with my family, I was not confident that I would ever be a profitable, prolific farmer.

I didn't have the mechanical knowledge to understand gears or transmissions, didn't have the skills to plow a perfect straight line, wasn't endowed with much biology knowledge on how to raise livestock, wasn't patient enough to battle chickens protecting their eggs, wasn't savvy enough to calculate seeds per acre, and wasn't cool and collected when seeing storm clouds approaching from the western horizon.

Freshmen had their required core classes that included either Algebra I or basic math. Algebra I, at that time, was taught by the high school football coach, who ran the curriculum similar to a football offense: if you don't fumble, you have a better chance to score (do well). Metaphorically speaking, I didn't handle the ball well and lost my hold on the football many times, resulting in barely passing Algebra I.

The next year, I had a choice of an easier math class, but instead I enrolled in the Algebra II class with a different teacher. Why I did that is beyond my comprehension, as the end result was another tough day at the ball park. Math was not my cup of tea, which I figured out after battling through geometry the following year. My destiny had nothing to do with becoming an accountant or engineer. Trigonometry and calculus were definitely crossed off my elective class list.

The football coach's wife was a teacher, and she taught a foreign language class that I found most enjoyable. In the first year of German I, when we were all assigned German names, I became Herr Rudolf, chosen in honor of my dad, who spelled his first name Rudolph. Close enough, I thought. The class appealed to me because of my family's German heritage. Plus, you never knew when you'd need to greet someone that spoke that language.

We repeated line after line of textbook High German or Low German and, to this day, some of that German language—and the songs we sang—are still tucked away in the back of my mind. We studied very basic sentences and greetings in German, and I can still say goodbye or hello, ask someone how they're doing, ask if they are feeling ill, tell someone to watch out, order potatoes off a menu, plus sing a couple of songs, one about a hat with three corners and another about a father who was a wandering man.

Because of that class, I branched out and joined German Club. Members would gather in the evenings for a soccer match, or go on a field trip to the Amana Colonies, where we observed German traditions and were treated to a lunch of wiener schnitzel, family style.

In my freshman science classes we learned about the Earth and rock formations. I think I should have paid more attention due to global warming and earthquakes looming large in today's news.

As sophomores, we advanced to comprehensive biology, which was much more entertaining because of all the things we got to dissect. Earthworms, frogs, and various other things were drenched in a smelly organic compound, which preserved the specimens so we could dissect them. Together with lab partners, we analyzed every part of the specimens' bodies and their reproductive systems. Hence, my parents never had to sit me down for a talk about 'the birds and bees.'

In our earlier high school years we participated in our school's science fairs. Some students excelled in these, and in showmanship, while others tried to make their projects just interesting enough to earn a passing grade. The goal of a significantly-underachieving science guy was always to be paired with a science guru, or at least someone who could ad lib their way through any questions tossed out by the judges. In my first science fair, my partner and I rigged together a hydroelectric power exhibit, achieving a good mark despite spilling water all over the gymnasium floor. Let's just say we put up a good front before the judges.

Debating in the classroom during junior and senior year speech classes was challenging, particularly if the subject matter was controversial. It was tough for my partner and me to debate the issue of smoking cigarettes and all its health complications. Obviously, we knew that smoking wasn't good for us, but to debate the issue on the pro-cigarette side and say that smoking cigarettes wasn't hazardous to your health, well, that was a no-win situation.

Language classes brought us closer to proper English usage and helped students break down sentences, which at times used graphed structures that were more complicated than math formulas. Many hours were devoted to subjects and predicates, adjectives, adverbs, and when to use who or whom. English, with words that sound the same but are spelled differently and have different meanings, or words that have silent consonants or vowels, can be brutal to students who don't have a firm grip on English usage.

The dictionary was a student's best friend. When I was in school, there were no computers with programs that offered spell checks, definitions, or how to use a word properly in a sentence. Calculators were permissible in some of the business classes and advanced math classes. To communicate with anyone outside of the classroom or school, we couldn't just pull out a cell phone like today. We had to march to the Principal's office and dial a telephone number, hoping there would be someone on the other end to answer the call.

We read *Giants in the Earth*, *The Scarlet Letter*, and *The Grapes of Wrath* in English literature classes, in preparation for quizzes and essays. Some books were better than others in holding my interest, but my first inclination was to peruse the sports books and the newspaper's sports page in the high school library to satisfy my reading fix, sometimes staying longer than I should and being tardy a time or two for my next class.

Gym classes were always part of the school's schedule. Students were introduced to fitness sports that weren't part of the school's varsity sport programs of football, cross country, baseball, basketball, track, and wrestling. Those fitness sports included fun things like wrestling mat football, wild and crazy dodge ball, handball, swimming, and running for health. I played countless handball games against others, wearing down the paint on the gymnasium walls.

Then there was the rope that hung from the rafters of the gymnasium ceiling. The assumed goal was for each student to climb the thick rope and touch the top of the metal rafter it was tied to. I never accomplished it, but some kids who had better agility skills, strength, and coordination just scooted up that rope like squirrels being chased by a dog.

Our physical education uniforms were supposed to be taken home and washed now and then, but mine got washed only when it felt too stiff and smelled awful. The shirts were reversible, so when one side got too dirty it was just turned inside out and used again. The real reason for reversible tops was so gym classes could be split into two teams, one team red and another gray, so we wouldn't be aiming dodge balls at our own teammates, which many did anyway.

We all looked forward to joining the long lunch lines in the middle of the school day, a welcome break. Students had their favorite meals; mine was chipped beef and gravy on toast. There were also wiener winks, peanut or plain butter sandwiches, sometimes goulash (but nothing like home), apple crisp desserts, cookies, chili, and cheese sticks.

I had a special attachment to the school lunch beverages, as it was my responsibility to fill the milk and chocolate milk dispensing machines in the serving line. That responsibility of lugging multi-gallon milk containers to the dispenser was my means of gaining a free meal. I earned this task due to my carelessness. My lunch tickets were always getting lost or left in my shirt pockets and run through Mom's washing machine. My parents finally drew the line; I had to work for my meals. It was a good experience, although I'm afraid I still have a consistent degree of absent-mindedness, plus I still lose things. Some things never change, no matter how old you get.

Over the course of our high school years, our class and the upper classes were fortunate to host students from foreign countries. The foreign exchange student program was going strong in the 1970s, and I can recall male and female students enrolling in our school from Japan, Sweden, Brazil, and Germany, plus a couple of other countries. One foreign student, a tall, muscular boy from Germany, had my utmost respect because he knew how to box, and he boxed very well. At times he'd slug me in the shoulder to get my attention and then smile a big, sheepish grin as if to say, "Welcome to my world." The guy wasn't timid in the least. My shoulder was sore for days afterwards, and I soon learned to anticipate his friendly punching moves whenever he had a question for me. I often wonder what paths these foreign exchange students took once they returned to their home countries.

High school was where my siblings and I took driver's education classes and learned to drive both stick shifts and automatic transmissions. We spent the first part of the class in the classroom, watching movies about driving rules and regulations, perusing graphic photographs and charts of crashes, and going over common-sense dos and don'ts.

Then three or four students packed into the driver's education vehicle and hit the pavement and gravel roads throughout the county. There were times the instructor would tell us, with little notice beforehand, to drive onto the road's shoulder without going into the ditch. Sometimes we would be required to steer into a shallow ditch and drive out of it. We'd drive uphill sometimes on slick, icy roads, where we shifted the manual transmission from high to low, or go down steep hills without grinding the gears, plus learn how to pump the brakes to avoid a runaway car. There were sessions on both angled parking and parallel parking.

On one trip, a semi-trailer truck was tailgating me and, for some reason, my first instinct was to brake as we approached the city limits. It scared the living daylights out of me when I glanced in the rearview mirror and saw that humongous semi-trailer truck driving close to my bumper. The instructor, perhaps seeing an imminent rear-end collision, calmly told me that putting on the brakes wasn't the right thing to do, in no uncertain terms, "at this particular time."

"Please go faster," he begged of me. Of course, I happily obliged him. The incident didn't seem to rattle him one bit, probably because he'd seen his share of student driving blunders and close calls.

Pep rallies prior to football and basketball games, complete with skits and cheers, helped break up the monotony of school. Guys dressed up like cheerleaders and cheerleaders dressed up as football players. The school's fight song, "Oh When the Saints Go Marching In" (our school teams were called the Saints), played on and on. Only twelve or so miles from our high school was Osage High School; its sports teams were called the Green Devils. Being so close to each other, there was always a heavenly rivalry between the Saints and the Green Devils.

Some school assemblies were more of a serious nature, such as a gathering to hear our draft lottery number called out for service to the Vietnam War; hashing over school policies; and hearing motivational speakers.

My biggest impression of high school, besides the pep rallies and colorful proms, that jump started my interest in creative writing, occurred in a small trailer classroom attached to the high school, occupied by Mr. Green, who taught English.

Up until his class I had coasted through high school, not really excelling in any class, just trying to get by. I was average, to say the least; I'm sure that's what the teachers told my parents at conferences and what was consistently reflected on my report cards.

One writing assignment Mr. Green dished out launched my writing career and gave me confidence. I wrote a story about the plight of a fictional, veteran professional football player who was fed up with the violent game of football. He had played Sunday after Sunday in every type of nasty weather, including downpours and snowstorms, and to him, it wasn't worth it anymore. He was at the end of his rope.

What I expected was a passing grade, but Mr. Green felt so moved by my story, he had me read it in front of the whole class. My confidence in my writing increased greatly, and my interest in creative writing flourished.

Another high school teacher saw some potential in my bookkeeping abilities, which I thought would be my career after high school. Doing well with adding machines and business ventures gave me the incentive to make the honor roll during my senior year and to enroll in a nearby business school after I graduated. Still, my urge to continue writing never wavered, and I went on a creative journey in newspaper journalism for 30 years.

Having inspirational and influential teachers helped all of my siblings, too, and guided them to their future careers. Several of my sisters went on to careers in the medical field. One sister became a teacher; another a secretary. Both brothers, who were mechanically inclined, joined the workforce after high school and are very successful. They all have their own stories about high school. Both served, or still serve, as volunteer firemen for their communities.

Were there some regrets about high school? Sure. It would have been nice to excel in a shop class, or to have said yes to the high school choir director when he asked me to sing in the choir. It would have been better to shoot for higher marks in regular classroom subjects, also, and perhaps participate in theater and more sports.

But the four years of high school went very fast as it was. High school graduation carried a great deal of prestige in my family. Some of the ceremonies took place outside in a city park, and others were held inside the school's gymnasium when weather didn't cooperate.

My siblings and I all had our senior graduation day photographs snapped in front of the lilac tree that grew in our backyard, right next to what we used as home plate during all our neighborhood baseball games. Relatives and neighbors came to the farm from miles away to help us celebrate. Mom made our favorite cake and served mints, salted peanuts, and sandwiches. It was like a family reunion or a block party, with tons of people bringing their own big families.

As the evening approached, some relatives stuck around to play cards while the person graduating opened up graduation gifts and cards. After more cake and well wishing, the celebration ended and the next step toward independence stared us in the face.

All of us relished our memories of the fastest four years in our respective histories. Time goes fast when you are growing up with nine siblings. Later, you go back home time and time again, to rehash, relive, and treasure those good times.

Who were your favorite high school teachers, and why?

The Poet

Thoughts just don't flow easy.
The mind struggles with the rhyme.
Verses seem to blend so sour
and one line is taking too much time.

How deep do the words bite?
Will people understand
the innermost thoughts you write,
with pen gripped in sweaty hands?

Poems are different, like snowflakes,
because no two should be the same.
One can speak of love, another hate,
encountered playing life's many games.

Will people tire of the feelings
thrust upon the pages?
Or will people read and marvel
and be impressed throughout the ages?

Will the poem dig deep,
stir a bad memory from days past?
Or will it strike a happy chord
of fond nostalgia that forever lasts?

Composing poems, like modeling clay,
needs to be molded into shape
so that it stands by itself,
leaving few thoughts to escape.

And if the poem moves
another to laugh or cry,
then all those heavy frustrations lift
and you simply give another poem a try.

Chapter Fifteen

In Their Words

It was my parents' 35th anniversary and one of the gifts they received was a scrapbook with memories written by their children. The scrapbook today is deteriorating, and it seems logical that it's a part of history that should be preserved for the oldest to youngest. Here are some shared memories, starting with the eldest sibling and on down.

"As I think back on my experiences on the farm, I realize how easy it is to take those experiences for granted. One tends to remember only those bad moments.

"One [memory] coming to mind is the time I was going out to the barn, where dad was milking cows in the evening. The barnyard, as I recall, was knee-deep in mud and manure. I went through the gate and about halfway across the yard before I noticed the bull, and the bull noticed me. I had never really had any fear of bulls until that day. I was sure that bull would kill me. (It was a Holstein bull and some say they can be the meanest animals on this earth.) I'm sure he was thinking about it as he edged closer and closer, and I could see his mean eyes looking at me. I started yelling for

Dad and it seemed an eternity before he heard me. But he came to my rescue and carried me to safety. I've always had respect for bulls from that day on.

"Another [memory] was the day Grandpa Hackenmiller died. (A widower, he stayed on the farm with our parents for a number of years.) I remember him as a quiet man who didn't say much except when he found us doing something we shouldn't be doing. One time I'd put a rope around Spit's (our pet dog) neck and he didn't like me doing that too well and made me take it off. I barely remember going to church with Grandpa in his car, and that he always had lemon drops and we would sneak into his room to get them out of his drawer.

"The day he died we were supposed to go somewhere for the day. It was a Sunday and I was excited. The next thing I knew, there were hundreds of people there in the yard (or so it seemed). I was six or seven at the time. I asked Mom when we were going and she said we weren't going because Grandpa had died.

"Many times, when I wanted to be alone, I would climb up to the roof of the shed and sit there for a while to contemplate and daydream. I think this is where I decided my future.

"The change of the seasons brings pleasant thoughts. It was so beautiful in the fall to see all the leaves turn colors and to smell the burning of raked leaves and to go out into the fields and pick up cornstalks for the livestock. I really enjoyed driving the tractor while the stalks were being picked up.

"It was beginning to get cooler. Then winter came with the first snowfall and the beautiful, white blanket. Every year we had to build a snowman or two. Even the blizzards were fun for me.

"It was somehow comforting to be inside the house—nice and warm—when there was a raging blizzard outside. It always felt good to stand on the old floor furnace to warm up, and to see the clothes rack standing over the furnace to dry the wash load. Of course, it was always a challenge to get to church, by tractor and wagon if necessary, as Mom insisted we must not miss Mass.

"Winter usually got pretty tiring, though, especially when it started thawing into spring. Spring was my least favorite season, with traces of snow and lots of mud. Although, it also did bring Easter, which meant that our Easter dresses and shoes came out. If we were lucky, we could get new dresses and shoes.

"Summer was great because that meant no school and time to bale hay and cut silage; time to drive the tractor again. And our neighbors would all get together to help each other harvest.

"What I didn't like was working in the huge garden. I don't know how Mom did it, and looking back, I'm extremely appreciative of all the hard work involved in that now. First to plant it, then to keep it clean, and then to get all the vegetables canned. I remember someone telling Mom once that she had the prettiest garden around. That made me feel very proud of my Mom.

"Summer always brought neighborhood gatherings and family reunions on our farm. If it wasn't jumping

into corn or soybeans from the rafters in the granary or corn shed, then it was piling up mounds of freshly-cut grass and making huts, framings for a house, or just jumping into the pile. Dad probably didn't like this as it would foul up the lawn mower later on that week when trying to mow through the mounds.

"I'm sure I could go on and on as I sit here and write, as memories flood in, but one thing is for sure: the farm life is what I wish everyone could experience.

"There were times when we could never go on any vacation because work on the farm would never stop. One has to admire Dad on being so dedicated to his job. Obviously, none of his children felt they could measure up to take over the farm. And of course, work was no easier for Mom, but we sure learned a lot to pass on to our own children. I hope we can do half as well."

"Both grandpas died when I was so young. The memory of them was so faint; however, the house that Grandpa and Grandma Michels had by the Osage, Iowa, fairgrounds remains vivid. I don't recall much about the inside of the house, but we sure had fun outside. I remember Mom and Dad leaving us with the grandparents and we got to ride in the wagon as Grandpa and Grandma planted oats, Grandma in her kerchief helping Grandpa.

"I guess I was pretty lucky when it came to chores. Before Mom needed me in the house, I followed Dad around all over the farm yard. Maybe I didn't do much but get in his way, but it was still fun being out with him. The only type of chores he gave me was to feed the calves their fresh milk from the pails after the milking.

Then Mom needed me to help in the house and I was given the job of washing the milkers with my sister.

"I still collected eggs and washed them, fed chickens, and drove the baler when Dad needed help. There were always enough drivers who could do a better job of driving because I tended to knock my passengers to their feet with my jerky starts. I'll even admit I never milked a cow.

"We'd spend afternoons within the corn crib, throwing ears of corn at the pigeons, or spend hours playing house in the house upstairs or in the brooder house when it wasn't in use. We certainly had imagination.

"We probably complained a lot about being so deprived compared to the city kids. In all actuality, I wouldn't change places with them. We always had friends, cousins, or neighbors, and siblings to do things with, if we didn't kill each other.

"Those co-ed softball games on Sunday nights were so much fun. I still get asked where I learned to play ball and I attribute it to all the times my brother and I played basketball and softball. All of our free time was spent on sports.

"Growing up in a family of twelve in my younger days could have seemed so awful and embarrassing— all those big Catholic family jokes to endure—but as I tell everyone now, I wouldn't change it for anything."

"Growing up on the farm really had its advantages. Where else would you learn the meaning of true work and responsibility? And the nice thing about it all was the fact that everyone had their own chores and stuck to them fairly well.

"I remember the girls taking turns with washing and drying dishes and sweeping the floor after every meal. We had a few squabbles from time to time.

"Dad would be in the hot fields during the day and it would be such a privilege to take out a jug of ice water to him. Riding in the wagon was another big thing, even if it was only a short distance. It was really fun growing up in a big family. We always had someone to be with. Mom and Dad always listened and helped us any way they could."

"We always seemed to make the best out of the things we had. Even the things we didn't have, we would find something else to use. For instance, my younger brother and I would use our older brother's shoes to pull our toy farm machinery. That worked good until Christmas that year when we both got real toy tractors.

"I remember how everyone would take ownership of a kitten after they were born. We would give the cat a name and it would be ours to care for. We did the same with newborn calves. It was always sad when our pet dogs and cats would die.

"We were excited when Dad took us to Osage and bought a brand-new Stingray bicycle. I remember how we always had to take turns riding it. We were also excited the day Mom would go shopping or rummaging and dad would go to a farm sale. We would wonder what they would come home with, whether it would be some clothes and candy for us kids, or a tractor or other piece of machinery for the farm.

"I enjoyed watching Dad make things. To me, there was nothing he couldn't handle, whether it was overhauling a tractor or remodeling the house.

"Driving a tractor all day long didn't bother me a bit. It gave me the satisfaction of helping Dad while I could think things over and daydream about school, cars, or whatever. Even though I'm living in a town now, I'll always consider the farm my real home."

"I remember one time getting into an argument with Mom about cleaning my room or something like that, and she told me if I thought it was so much work, try cooking three meals a day for twelve people sometime.

"She was right, and that also included laundry work, garden work, house work, farm work, school work, church work, raising ten kids, and then going to work as a waitress for two or more days a week.

"I can remember, also, how I thought about Dad and that he was the smartest man in the world. It always amazed me how he always knew when to plant corn, bale hay, sell the pigs, treat sick animals, or fix machinery.

"But I guess what sticks in my mind most were the simple things, like that half-stick of gum he gave us that would dry our tears, and the waiting and anticipation at the end of our driveway for the folks to come home, maybe with treats for the children.

"I always reflect back on my life on the farm, almost every day. And always will."

"Companionship was never a problem. There was always someone to ride bikes to the creek, play a game of ball, or give me a few pushes on the tire swing that Dad made for us.

"I recall sitting on the see-saw, licking our home-made popsicles, and talking with one another. Or sledding for hours on end after Dad would pile up snow with his tractor and loader after a big snowfall.

"Of course, we didn't always get along. I think Mom and Dad both knew that an argument or two was in the forecast for each day. Yet bad feelings never seemed to last for more than a few hours. How many times did we fight over two bikes that five or six of us wanted to ride at the same time, or to try out something first, or who was going to get what Mom came home with from rummage sales?

"Even though we were all scattered over the farm after breakfast, we could count on seeing each other at dinner and supper again. Someone would always be spilling a pitcher of milk or get too much of the giggles.

"The common slogan—a family that stays together, prays together—really seemed to hold true for us. From the days I can remember, Mom and Dad never let us lose sight of our prayerful duties."

"Living on the farm was full of adventure. All we needed was a creative mind and, with ten kids in the family, someone was bound to come up with something.

"With so many of us, though, you were bound to find an ally in the group. Sometimes we helped each other fight their individual battles; sometimes we just lent a sympathetic ear. Either way we were never alone.

"There were times, though, when I preferred to be alone; I'd wander into a peaceful hideaway where I could do some serious thinking, or just daydream.

"While it may be possible to describe what an average family does on a farm, it is impossible to define the feelings that pass between the members of that family. That feeling is a very personal thing, something only understood by the members it touches."

"It was never a dull moment growing up on the farm with six sisters and three brothers. It wasn't always fun and games, though. I can remember the cold, rainy Saturday mornings Mom would get us up bright and early to butcher the chickens. How we moaned and groaned, but it was always worth it to have a big chicken dinner every Sunday.

"We were always fortunate to have our own ice pond in the field. Unfortunately, by the time we walked all the way out there to it, our fingers, nose, and toes were so cold and numb we had to turn right back home.

"I know there were times when I wondered what it would be like to be an only child. Not having to wear your older sister's clothes or to share your belongings. But now, looking back, I could never replace the fun memories our family has had together."

"They say that true happiness can never be reached, but I know that I am as happy as can be when we're all together. We've maybe gone one step further than some families by giving in a little and contentedly living with the results.

"It is so nice to see that our family is still growing, with in-laws and grandchildren we've come to know and *love. Being the youngest, I feel I've gotten to know my siblings better, and I'm very grateful for that."*

How would you describe your own childhood?

Chapter Sixteen

Moving On

After high school, it was time to begin another phase in life: leaving the nest. Granted, it took many years for that to happen as the family grew in numbers. Eventually, though, one child after another left to embark on educational opportunities and careers, whittling our family household numbers slowly to just two, Mom and Dad.

Some of my siblings found jobs or went to college; all pursued various occupations. We followed our dreams, or temporarily parked our ambitions to make ends meet so that down the road we could achieve our life goals.

No longer were the two parents scrambling like crazy to get their children out of the house and onto the school bus. Meals planned for twelve slowly reduced to dinner for two. Family outings that once required exquisite planning became more free-spirited adventures by the two parents. Perhaps there would be a special chance for that fishing trip to Minnesota, which had been delayed until the children were grown and on their own. It was only when Dad and Mom sold the dairy operation, which always consumed a good portion of their time, that they, too, would find time to travel.

Other new opportunities soon came to be, including dining at some fine restaurants, feasting on steaks that didn't come from their own freezer. While we were all getting a taste of our own independence, our parents were enjoying quiet times and getting to know each other all over again, sometimes over a candlelight dinner.

The folks could now do more activities with other parents whose children had also left the nest, such as going to a movie or theatrical performance. Our parents could go back to school, become officers of various organizations, and do more volunteer work simply because they had more time for themselves.

Ideally, that's what we children think our parents deserve—this time to themselves. But in reality, most parents never stop loving their children and so continue to harbor interest in their children's daily interests and hobbies. They find themselves immersed in their children's lives because they simply don't want to let go. Parents treasure visits or phone calls from their children and get insulted if they find out you were in town and didn't stop to say hello.

Parents also become the main cheering section and fan club for their grandchildren's athletic events, dances, and piano or vocal recitals. They provide the means of transportation to and from school or recreational activities when both parents can't get away from their jobs.

It is safe to conclude that the core of family life never really exits the nest; a huge world exists out there, but only if family remains a big part of the picture.

My siblings, like many others in large families, had the utmost respect and gratitude for our parents, and can only marvel at how the two of them were able to pull through together when the going got tough: when there weren't enough dollars to stretch for all the bills that needed to be paid; when hail destroyed the field crops and gardens; when school tuitions depleted their savings; when the flu bug came calling and had the whole family down for days; when the clutches blew out on family cars and tractors; when the hens stopped laying eggs and the milk check was minimal; when the sows decided to give birth on the coldest day of the year.

We, in turn, are extremely grateful to them, and so we find it hard to completely leave the nest, always finding our way home on a getaway weekend to rekindle, savor, and listen to the stories passed down and around our parents' dinner table.

Maybe over a steaming hot plate of goulash, which sounds really good right now.

The End

Mom's Recipes

Apple Spaghetti Salad

Cook 2 cups of small ring spaghetti as directed, drain and set aside to cool. Peel and cube 6 apples. You may leave some of the red peel on for color.

Make dressing in a double boiler: 2 cups powdered sugar, ½ cup lemon juice, and 4 eggs. Beat eggs, then add juice and sugar. Cook and stir until thick.

Cool mixture, then pour into large bowl and add fruit and spaghetti. Mix thoroughly. Let stand 12 to 24 hours. Just before serving, mix in one 8-ounce carton of Cool Whip.

Serves 6-8.

Copper Pennies

Slice 5 cups of carrots and put in a sauce pan. Add a small amount of water and cook for up to 10 minutes. Drain carrots and put in a large mixing bowl. Add the following ingredients to the hot carrots: 1 medium onion, sliced thin; 1 medium green pepper, chopped fine; 1 cup of celery, chopped; ¾ cup vinegar; ½ cup salad oil; 2/3 cup sugar; 1 tsp. Worcestershire sauce; 1 can tomato soup; ½ tsp. salt; 1 tsp. prepared mustard. Refrigerate overnight.

Serves 6-8.

Chili

Brown up to 3 pounds of hamburger and drain. Put into a large, heavy kettle and add: 1 gallon chili beans, 1 gallon tomato sauce, 1 46-ounce can tomato juice, ½ cup brown sugar, 1 tsp. salt, ½ tsp. pepper, 1 heaping tbsp. chili powder, and 1 diced onion. Simmer, stirring occasionally, for three or four hours. Freezes well.

Serves 10-12.

Goulash

1½ pounds of hamburger, 1 small can mushrooms, 1 small can tomato paste, 1 cup cold water, ¼ cup diced green pepper, ½ tsp. pepper, ¼ tsp. oregano, 4 cups cooked macaroni, 1 diced medium onion, ¼ tsp. garlic powder, 1 tsp. salt.

Brown hamburger and onion together in Dutch oven or deep skillet. Add seasonings and other ingredients and mix. Bake one hour at 350 degrees. In last 15 minutes, add shredded mozzarella or American cheese on top.

Serves 4-6.

Another Goulash

1 cup uncooked macaroni; 1 pound lean ground beef; ½ pound fresh sliced mushrooms; 1 cup chopped onion; 1 clove minced garlic; 1 6-ounce can of no-salt tomato paste; ¾ cup water; 1 cup low-sodium ketchup; 1 small bay leaf; 1 tsp. sugar; ½ tsp. pepper; ¼ tsp. dried oregano; ¼ tsp. chopped basil.

Cook macaroni according to package directions, omitting salt. Drain and set aside. Brown beef with mushrooms, onion, and garlic. Pour off fat and add in remaining ingredients. Simmer gently about 15 minutes. Add cooked, drained macaroni. Simmer five minutes more. Remove bay leaf and serve.

Serves 4-6.

Marcella's Homemade Bread

Bring 2 cups milk to the boiling point (scald, don't boil). Turn off heat. Add ¼ cup butter and let it melt. Add 2 cups of cold water and one heaping tbsp. of salt. Cool to lukewarm.

After cooling, use mixer and start mixing in flour, a little at a time, until dough is too stiff for mixer. About halfway through, add one heaping tbsp. of dry yeast (not quick rising) and one heaping tbsp. sugar. Continue adding flour and mixing by hand until you have used about half of a 5 lb. bag of flour. Put in a large greased bowl.

Cover the bowl and let it rise until it doubles in size. Butter hands and knead it down again. Let it rise until doubled again. Make into loaves - the recipe makes about four good-sized loaves. Let the dough rise in the greased tins.

Bake at 360 for about 35 minutes. Move the loaves around in the oven so that they will bake evenly. Remove from the tins immediately and put on the cooling rack. Butter the tops of bread. Cool completely before freezing.

List some of your favorite family recipes?

This is Chuck Hackenmiller's fourth self-published book. Now retired, he served as photographer, journalist and editor of Iowa and Nebraska newspaper publications. He and his wife recently moved to Lincoln, Nebraska to be closer to their own family.

Disclaimer: All writing, poems, and prose in this book are the work of the author except for my siblings' memories, the songs listed, and the poem named "Farmer's Request," which is by an unknown author.